WHEN DID IT HAPPEN?

A SIMON AND SCHUSTER
color illustrated question and answer book

WHEN DID IT HAPPEN?

Placing important events, people, inventions
—and more—in time

Simon and Schuster Books for Young Readers
Published by Simon & Schuster Inc.
New York London Toronto Sydney Tokyo Singapore

First English language edition published in Great Britain
by Grisewood and Dempsey Ltd.
Text Copyright © 1985 Grisewood and Dempsey Ltd
Illustrations copyright © 1985 Grisewood and Dempsey Ltd/
Librairie Hachette/Arnoldo Mondadori Editore S.p.A.

Simon and Schuster
Books for Young Readers
Published by Simon & Schuster Inc.
Simon & Schuster Building
1230 Avenue of the Americas
New York, New York 10020

10 9 8 7 6 5 4 3 2 1   (Pbk) 10 9 8 7 6 5 4 3 2 1

SIMON AND SCHUSTER BOOKS FOR YOUNG READERS and colophon are
trademarks of Simon & Schuster Inc.
ISBN 0-671-72497-5 (Pbk)
ISBN 0-671-60426-0   ISBN 0-671-60428-7 (lib. bdg.)
D.L.TO:847-1990
Printed in Spain by Artes Gráficas Toledo, S.A.

Authors
Neil Ardley
Beverley Birch
Jean Cooke
Mark Lambert
James Muirden
Theodore Rowland-Entwistle
Brian Williams
Jill Wright

Artists
Norma Burgin/John Martin & Artists
Jeffrey Burn
Geraint Derbyshire/John Martin & Artists
Jim Dugdale/Jillian Burgess
Ron Jobson/Jillian Burgess
Jerry Malone/Tudor Art Agency
Bernard Robinson/Tudor Art Agency
Mike Roffe
Mike Saunders/Jillian Burgess
Michael Youens

CONTENTS

SCIENCE AND TECHNOLOGY

HOW PEOPLE LIVE

TRANSPORTATION

PLANET EARTH

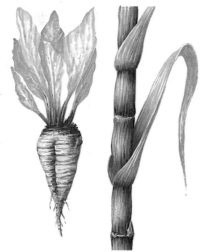

PLANTS AND ANIMALS

▶WHEN DID LIFE ON
EARTH BEGIN?

**The first living things were
bacteria, which appeared on
earth about 3.5 billion years
ago.**

Life began on earth in
conditions that would have
been fatal to modern living
things. The atmosphere
contained many poisonous
chemicals. There was little or
no oxygen, and strong
ultraviolet radiation from the
sun penetrated the seas.

It was in such conditions
that life seems to have begun.
The seas were a rich "soup" of
chemicals, and it is thought
that the molecules of the
chemicals began to join up to

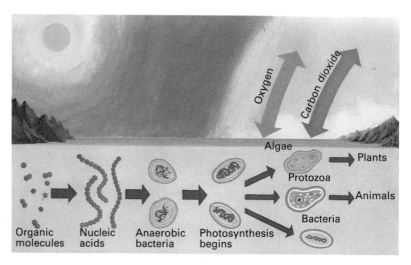

form larger molecules. Among
these were the nucleic acids
(DNA and RNA) on which all
modern life forms are based.
Fatty membranes developed
round the nucleic acid
molecules, thus forming the

first primitive cells. Successful
cells grew and multiplied.
Eventually, they gave rise to
the first bacterialike
organisms. Some of these
began to make their own food
by photosynthesis.

▶WHICH ARE THE
OLDEST-KNOWN PLANTS?

**The first plants were blue-
green algae. Their fossil
remains have been found in
rocks over three billion years
old.**

As photosynthetic bacteria
evolved, they began releasing
oxygen into the atmosphere.
High in the atmosphere, the
harsh ultraviolet radiation
from the sun turned the
oxygen into ozone. This
formed a layer through which
the most harmful radiation
could not pass. As a result life
in the seas below was able to
develop further.

The oldest-known fossil
plant comes from 3.2 billion-
year-old rocks in South Africa.

It is a single-celled blue-green
alga called *Archaeosphaeroides*.

Blue-green algae still exist.
In some parts of the world they
form colonies that produce
limestone. They build it up in
layers to form cushion-shaped
structures known as

stromatolites (shown here).
Such colonies existed over two
billion years ago. The oldest-
known fossil stromatolites are
2.8 billion years old. The inset
illustration shows the layers
inside a fossil stromatolite.

▼ WHICH ARE THE OLDEST-KNOWN ANIMALS?

The first animals probably appeared at the same time as the first plants. But the first animals that we know of for certain are worms, jellyfish and similar animals that existed over 700 million years ago.

The first animals were almost certainly single-celled types, or protozoans. But we have no fossil evidence of such animals. In turn, protozoans gave rise to simple, many-celled animals. We have no real idea of what these animals looked like.

The first fossil evidence comes from the Ediacara Hills in Australia, where there are fossil-bearing rocks over 700 million years old. The fossil animals contained in these rocks are known as the Ediacara fauna.

The picture shows reconstructions of some of the Ediacara animals. *Ediacara* and *Kimbrella* were jellyfish, and *Cyclomedusa* was one of their bottom-living relatives. Sea pens were also relatives of the jellyfish. *Spriggina* and *Dickinsonia* were wormlike animals. *Tribrachium* was a primitive relative of modern sea urchins and starfish.

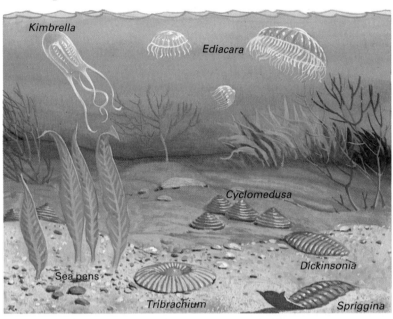

Kimbrella
Ediacara
Cyclomedusa
Dickinsonia
Sea pens
Tribrachium
Spriggina

▲ WHEN DO FOSSILS FORM?

A fossil is formed when all or part of an animal or plant becomes included in rock. Usually it is the hard parts, such as bones or shells.

Scientists believe that over 9.8 billion species have existed since life began. But only a small number of these (about 800,000) have left fossil remains. This is because the process of fossilization needs special conditions.

A typical fossil is formed from hard material, such as bone. When an animal dies (1), its soft parts decay rapidly (2). If the animal died in water, the bones may then become quickly buried in a sediment, such as particles of clay or limestone. As time passes, the sediment is covered by other layers of sediment and hardens into rock (3). At the same time, the tiny holes or pores in the bone may be filled with minerals from the sediment. Or the bones may dissolve and be entirely replaced by minerals. This leaves stone copies, or casts, of the original bones in molds formed by the surrounding rock. Finally, over millions of years, the rocks may be pushed out of the sea to form land. When the rocks are eroded, the fossil bones are eventually exposed (4).

▼WHEN DID ANIMALS WITH SHELLS APPEAR?

The Cambrian period marks the start of the main fossil record. This is because about 600 million years ago animals with hard parts (shells) began to evolve.

Precambrian animals were all soft-bodied creatures and were therefore very vulnerable to predators. Animals that could protect themselves with hard shells had a great advantage.

Many animals with limestone shells lived in the Cambrian seas. There were gastropod mollusks (sea snails) and bivalves (mollusks with shells divided into two hinged parts, or valves). Brachiopods, or lamp shells, were very common. Also there were primitive echinoderms ("spiny skinned" animals), which were the ancestors of modern starfish and sea urchins.

Other animals, too, had developed hard outer coverings. These were the first arthropods (animals with jointed limbs, e.g. crabs and insects), among which were the trilobites.

▼WHEN DID THE FIRST FISHES APPEAR?

Sometime during the Ordovician period, the first vertebrates (backboned animals) evolved. These were the jawless fishes or ostracoderms ("shell skins").

We do not know how the first vertebrates evolved. But it is possible that they arose from a group of echinoderms.

Most ostracoderms were less than 20 inches long. Their mouths were just holes or slits through which they could suck water and food particles. There were three main groups. Cephalaspids (e.g. *Hemicyclaspis*) were sluggish fishes with flattened heads that were covered by a bony head-shield. Pteraspids (e.g. *Pteraspis*) also had head-shields, but these were made up of several bony plates.

Anaspids (e.g. *Jamoytius*) were the smallest ostracoderms. They had no head-shields, but many of them had bodies covered in thick scales. Anaspids may have been the ancestors of lampreys and hags, the modern jawless fishes.

▲WHICH ANIMALS LIVED IN THE ANCIENT SEAS?

During the Cambrian, Ordovician and Silurian periods the seas teemed with all kinds of invertebrate (non-backboned) animals.

The picture shows some of the animals that lived in the sea during the Ordovician period (530–440 million years ago). Trilobites (1) were very common. They were between an inch and two feet long. Most of them crawled about the sea bed, feeding on soft-bodied creatures.

Earlier groups of animals also spread. There were sponges (8), jellyfish (7) and various kinds of coral (9). Several types of echinoderm included cystoids (4), crinoids, or sea lilies (5), and echinoids, or urchins (6). Brachiopods (2) were still common, as were gastropod and bivalve mollusks. There was also another mollusk group, the nautiloids (10). These were squidlike animals with long, conical shells, ancestors of the ammonites and the modern squids and octopuses.

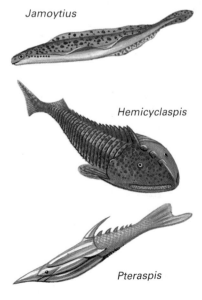

Jamoytius

Hemicyclaspis

Pteraspis

▼WHEN DID THE FIRST JAWED FISHES APPEAR?

The first fishes with movable jaws appeared during the Silurian period, about 420 million years ago. But their jaws were very different from those of the sharks and bony fishes, which appeared soon afterwards.

The first jawed fishes were the placoderms ("plate skins"). Their heads were covered in heavy armor plates and the jaws were formed from two hinged plates.

The early placoderms were fairly small. But by the Devonian period there were giants. *Dunkleosteus* was over 30 feet long and it would have been possible for a human to stand inside its open jaws.

The Devonian period is often called the Age of Fishes. Jawless fishes and placoderms were both present. In addition, more advanced fishes were starting to appear. Among these were the sharks, such as *Cladoselache*, with skeletons made of cartilage. Bony fishes also appeared at this time. *Climatius* was a member of a

group known as spiny sharks, so called because there was a spine at the front edge of each fin. It is thought that spiny sharks evolved from anaspid fishes and gave rise to all the later bony fishes.

Bony fishes are divided into two main groups. The lobe-fins include the coelacanth and the extinct rhipidistians (see page 14). They get their name from the fact that their fins are supported on fleshy lobes. All other fishes belong to the ray-fins. *Cheirolepis* is the earliest known ray-fin.

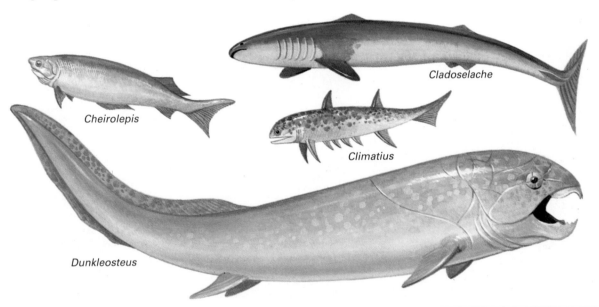

Cladoselache

Cheirolepis

Climatius

Dunkleosteus

►WHEN DID PLANTS FIRST GROW ON THE LAND?

During the Silurian and Devonian periods the land began to be invaded. The first colonizers were plants.

Mosses and similar plants may have invaded the land during the Ordovician or early Silurian periods. But no fossil remains of such plants have been found. The earliest land plants seem to have been a group known as psilophytes. These were simple plants with

no true roots or leaves, but their stems were upright and contained water-conducting cells. The oldest known psilophyte is *Cooksonia*, fossils of which have been found in late Silurian rocks (400 million years old). *Zosterophyllum* was a Devonian psilophyte that grew stems up to 12 inches high.

Clubmosses also existed during the Devonian period. Plants such as *Baragwanathia* and *Drepanophycus* were the ancestors of the modern clubmosses and of the giant Carboniferous types.

Cooksonia

Zosterophyllum

Ichthyostega

Hylonomus

**The first amphibians
appeared in the late Devonian
period. They are thought to
have evolved from lobe-
finned fishes.**

During the Devonian period
there was a group of lobe-fins
known as the rhipidistians.
These fishes became extinct
about 250 million years ago,
during the Permian period.
Before they disappeared, they
probably gave rise to the
amphibians.

Rhipidistians, like other
fishes, had fins for swimming.
But their fins were supported
on fleshy lobes that could
easily have been used for
crawling. Some rhipidistians
may have been tempted to
crawl out of their ponds to feed
on the increasing amount of
plant food on land. Young,
light-bodied fish may have
found this easier than older
ones. Gradually, the more
successful crawlers developed
stronger limbs and spent more
and more time on land,
eventually giving rise to the
first true amphibians.

▲WHICH PLANTS FORMED THE CARBONIFEROUS FORESTS?

**The swampy forests of the
Carboniferous period were
dominated by clubmosses,
including both small and
giant kinds. In addition,
there were large numbers of
horsetails, some of which
also grew into huge trees.
Ferns, tree ferns and seed
ferns were abundant.**

The origins of the various
groups of Carboniferous plants
are uncertain. They probably
evolved from the psilophytes.
But no linking fossils have
been found.

Like modern clubmosses
and ferns, the Carboniferous
plants needed moisture to help
them produce their spores. So
they lived around swamps and
ponds, forming vast swamp
forests.

Club mosses varied in size
from small types that
resembled modern clubmosses
to huge trees over 100 feet
high, such as *Lepidodendron*,
Bothrodendron and *Sigillaria*.
On the left of the picture are
(from left to right) a

Lepidodendron, two *Sigillaria*
and a tree called *Calamites*.
This last type was a giant
horsetail. *Sphenophyllum*, a
much smaller horsetail, is
shown in the bottom-left
corner.

The Carboniferous period is
often called the Age of Ferns.
This is because there are many
fernlike fossils in coal, which
was formed at that time. There
were indeed a large number of
ferns, including tree ferns, but
many of the fossils belonged to
seed ferns. Like modern
conifers, these reproduced by
seeds rather than spores.

▼WHICH ANIMALS LIVED IN CARBONIFEROUS FORESTS?

The dominant animals during the Carboniferous period were the amphibians.

Carboniferous amphibians belonged to two main groups. The labyrinthodonts, such as *Ichthyostega*, were fishlike animals with short, but useful, limbs. Some were large animals. *Ichthyostega* was about three feet long and others were even larger.

Lepospondyls, on the other hand, were generally smaller. Most spent all their lives in water and had small or non-existent limbs. *Ophiderpeton* was a snakelike lepospondyl.

The labyrinthodonts dominated the scene. *Eogyrinus*, one of the later types, was 16 feet long and lived entirely in water. It fed voraciously on fish. Competition from such giants may have caused some of the smaller amphibians to leave the water. Such animals may have developed tougher skins and given rise to the first reptiles.

Eogyrinus

Ophiderpeton

Rhipidistians

▲WHEN DID REPTILES FIRST APPEAR?

The first reptiles evolved during the late Carboniferous period. During the Permian period (280–225 million years ago) they took over the land.

The earliest known reptile is *Hylonomus*, fossils of which have been found in late Carboniferous rocks. It measures between eight inches and three feet in length, and it probably fed on insects. It seems to have made its home in old tree stumps.

Hylonomus belonged to a group known as cotylosaurs, or stem reptiles, so called because they probably gave rise to all the later reptiles. Other stem reptiles included the flesh-eating *Limnoscelis*, and its smaller relative *Labidosaurus*. The largest stem reptiles were the plant-eating pareiasaurs, such as *Scutosaurus* and *Pareiasaurus*. They were protected by an armor of bony knobs and were over 10 feet long. By the end of the Permian period all the stem reptiles had disappeared.

▼WHICH REPTILES HAD "SAILS?"

The dominant group of reptiles during the Permian period were the mammal-like reptiles. Some were very strange animals with "sails."

The mammal-like reptiles are so called because they possessed some of the features of mammals. The earliest types were the pelycosaurs. Among these were the "sail-backs," such as *Dimetrodon* and *Edaphosaurus*. *Dimetrodon* was a large, flesh-eating pelycosaur about 11 feet long. Its "sail" may have been used to help control its body temperature. If the sail was turned sideways on to the sun, the blood running through it heated up. If the animal needed to cool down, it would have found some shade and turned so that the front edge of the "sail" faced the sun.

Later mammal-like reptiles varied from huge, ferocious creatures, such as the gorgonopsian *Lycaenops*, to smaller, doglike cynodonts. It was probably the cynodonts that gave rise to the first true mammals.

Dimetrodon

▼WHAT WAS THE AGE OF REPTILES?

The history of life on earth is divided into three eras. The Mesozoic, or "middle life," era is known as the Age of Reptiles.

The geological timescale below shows the history of living things based on the ages of the rocks in which their fossil remains are found. There are three main eras. The boundaries between the eras mark the times when major changes took place. Many groups of animals became extinct at these times. Each era is divided into periods.

The Paleozoic, or "ancient life," era saw the evolution of the invertebrate groups, the fishes, the amphibians and the first reptiles. The Mesozoic, or "middle life," era was dominated completely by the reptiles, which took over the land, the seas and the air. The Cenozoic, or "new life," era saw the rise of the mammals and still continues today.

▼WHICH REPTILES DID DINOSAURS EVOLVE FROM?

During the Triassic period there existed a group of reptiles called the thecodonts. Some of these began to run on their hind legs. Their descendants were the dinosaurs.

The thecodonts gave rise to all the ruling reptiles, or archosaurs. These included not only the dinosaurs but also the pterosaurs (flying reptiles) and crocodiles.

There were several types of thecodont. Many were crocodilelike creatures with limbs that were held out sideways. Others, however, had limbs that were placed underneath their bodies, enabling them to run more swiftly. Some of these developed large hind legs and short front legs, and began to use only their hind legs for running. From this type arose the dinosaurs, which also typically ran on their hind legs. Even those that returned to walking on all four legs tended to have larger hind legs than front legs.

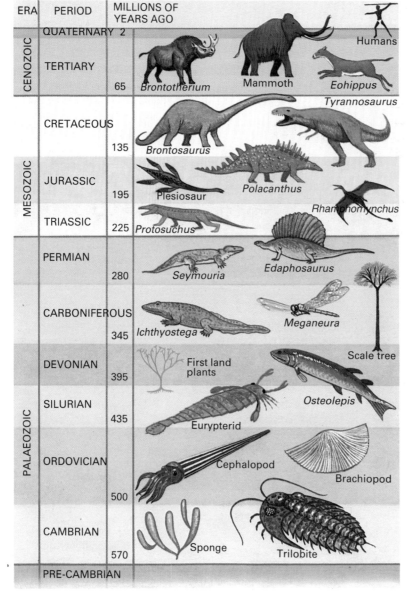

ERA	PERIOD	MILLIONS OF YEARS AGO
CENOZOIC	QUATERNARY	2
	TERTIARY	65
MESOZOIC	CRETACEOUS	135
	JURASSIC	195
	TRIASSIC	225
PALAEOZOIC	PERMIAN	280
	CARBONIFEROUS	345
	DEVONIAN	395
	SILURIAN	435
	ORDOVICIAN	500
	CAMBRIAN	570
	PRE-CAMBRIAN	

Brontotherium • Mammoth • Eohippus • Humans • Tyrannosaurus • Brontosaurus • Polacanthus • Plesiosaur • Rhamphorhynchus • Protosuchus • Seymouria • Edaphosaurus • Ichthyostega • Meganeura • Scale tree • First land plants • Osteolepis • Eurypterid • Cephalopod • Brachiopod • Sponge • Trilobite

Euparkeria

▼WHICH DINOSAURS HAD LARGE PLATES?

Among the strangest dinosaurs were the stegosaurs, which were equipped with plates.

The stegosaurs, such as *Stegosaurus*, evolved during the Jurassic period. But they were not particularly successful and many questions about them remain unanswered.

Stegosaurus is usually thought of as a plant-eater. But it had a very small head and mouth, so it would have taken *Stegosaurus* a long time to eat enough plant material to keep it alive. Some scientists think therefore that *Stegosaurus* may have lived on carrion (dead animals).

The plates are often thought of as armor. But *Stegosaurus* would still have been very vulnerable, particularly along its flanks. Another idea is that the plates may have been used to warm or cool the blood.

The spiked tail of *Stegosaurus* is another mystery. *Stegosaurus* could not have flailed the tail from side to side. So this "weapon" does not seem to have been very useful.

▼WHICH WERE THE LARGEST DINOSAURS?

The largest dinosaurs were the sauropods, such as *Brontosaurus*. But despite their size they were probably gentle animals. Their size was merely a form of defense against flesh-eating dinosaurs.

The huge size of a sauropod is hard to imagine. *Diplodocus*, the longest of them all, measured 80 feet from head to tail. It appears to have had a "relay station" – a swelling in the spinal nerve cord – to help its brain control the rear end of its body. *Brachiosaurus*, the most massive of the sauropods, is thought to have weighed between 80 and 100 tons.

Sauropods appeared in the Triassic period and became very common during the Jurassic period. They were plant-eaters and probably spent their time eating leaves, reaching up to the highest branches. Their great size probably deterred most predators, but they may have been able to defend themselves with their powerful legs and tails.

▼WHICH DINOSAURS HAD HORNS?

The horned dinosaurs, or ceratopsians, appeared during the Cretaceous period. The horns and head-shields must have been useful protection against the fierce carnosaurs.

The horned dinosaurs were a very successful group that survived right to the end of the Cretaceous period. Primitive types included the relatively small *Protoceratops*. This had a head-shield, but no horn, and was about six feet long. Later types developed single horns at the front of the head-shields, and additional horns at the back.

Among the largest of the advanced ceratopsians was *Triceratops*, which was about 26 feet long. The horns and head-shield almost certainly provided protection for the animal's head and neck. The horns may have been used in "battles" between rival males. They could have locked horns and engaged in a pushing match to establish which of the two was the stronger.

Brontosaurus

Triceratops

Protoceratops

Stegosaurus

▶WHICH DINOSAURS
LOOKED LIKE ARMORED
TANKS?

**The most heavily armored
dinosaurs were the
ankylosaurs. Some of them
must have been almost
impossible to attack and kill.**

The ankylosaurs appeared in
the early Cretaceous period.
They may have been
descendants of the stegosaurs,
which also had armor. Among
the early types was
Polacanthus. Its relatively light
armor consisted of two rows of
tall spiky cones down its neck
and part of its back. There
were also bony knobs and
plates around its hips and tail.

The later ankylosaurs were
all squat animals that bristled
with armored spines and
knobs. *Euoplocephalus*
(formerly also known as
Ankylosaurus) was about 13
feet long. It was half the length
of *Stegosaurus,* but weighed
twice as much. The whole of
the upper surface of its body
was protected by closely
packed bony plates
strengthened with bony knobs.
Its best method of defense was
probably to drop onto its belly
and wait for the attacker to
give up and go away. If
necessary, it could probably
have swung its massive clublike tail from side to side. But
it probably could not swing its
tail very accurately.

Ankylosaurs appear to have
been fairly common during the
Cretaceous period, so their
armor was presumably very
effective. One of the best-
protected ankylosaurs was
Scolosaurus. Its body was
covered in large spines. The
two largest spines were on the
end of its clublike tail.

▲WHEN DID FLESH-
EATING DINOSAURS
APPEAR?

**Throughout the history of the
dinosaurs there were flesh-
eating types. The largest and
fiercest appeared in the
Jurassic and Cretaceous
periods.**

The early flesh-eating
dinosaurs, or theropods,
were very similar to their
thecodont ancestors.
Coelophysis was a Triassic type
that measured 10 feet long. It
belonged to the group of

lightly built theropods called
coelurosaurs. Jurassic
coelurosaurs included the
chicken-sized *Compsognathus*
and the six-foot-long *Coelurus.*

The larger, heavier
theropods are known as
carnosaurs. The most massive
and fearsome types existed
during the Jurassic and
Cretaceous periods. The
largest were the Jurassic
megalosaurs, such as
Megalosaurus and *Allosaurus*
and the Cretaceous
tyrannosaurids, such as
Tyrannosaurus.

Anatosaurus

Ornitholestes

Compsognathus

Deinonychus

◀WHICH DINOSAURS COULD RUN THE FASTEST?

The fastest dinosaurs were the ornithomimids. These were egg-eating dinosaurs that raided the nests of other dinosaurs.

The ornithomimids were a group of Cretaceous coelurosaurs. Unlike their flesh-eating relatives, they had no teeth. They appear to have fed by sucking out the contents of the eggs of other dinosaurs,

Ornithomimids had three-fingered "hands" that were probably used for scraping away sticks or sand to find nests. They had very long hind legs and were obviously very agile. Scientists have calculated that *Ornithomimus* could have run at speeds of up to 50 miles an hour. However, studies of its footprints have shown that it usually traveled at less than 12 miles an hour. It probably used its high-speed running ability only in real emergencies.

◀WHICH WAS THE LARGEST FLESH-EATER?

The largest known flesh-eating land animal that has ever lived is *Tyrannosaurus*. It stood over 16 feet high and measured 46 feet from head to tail. Its teeth were six inches long.

Tyrannosaurus lived in North America during the late Cretaceous period. It is often thought of as one of the most terrifying animals that has ever lived. But its reputation is probably exaggerated.
   Like other carnosaurs,

Tyrannosaurus and its relatives ran on their hind legs. But tyrannosaurids had tiny front limbs that were almost useless. They relied on their massive jaws for catching prey. The hind legs of these animals were set quite far apart. As a result they probably waddled along rather slowly. Most other animals would have been able to escape fairly easily and so tyrannosaurids probably preyed on sick and wounded animals, and may have lived on carrion for much of the time. So *Tyrannosaurus* and its relatives were probably not the dominant predators.

▲WERE DINOSAURS WARM-BLOODED?

Mammals and birds are described as being warm-blooded animals. Reptiles are described as cold-blooded. Dinosaurs were reptiles, but some evidence indicates that they may have been warm-blooded.

A warm-blooded animal produces the heat that it needs from inside its body, and can maintain an almost constant body temperature. A cold-blooded animal, on the other

hand, relies on heat from outside its body to keep it warm. Its body temperature therefore rises and falls with the temperature of its surroundings.
   Cold-blooded animals tend to be relatively small. Many dinosaurs, however, were large. Cold-blooded animals of this size would have been rather sluggish and they would have had difficulty in regaining lost heat quickly enough. But even the largest dinosaurs appear to have been able to move fairly swiftly for quite long periods of time.

Cold-blooded animals are active during the day. At night they cannot get warm enough to move about very much. The coelurosaur *Deinonychus*, however, seems to have been a night-hunter – it had keen sight and an acute sense of smell. But to hunt at night, without the sun's warmth, it must have been warm-blooded.
   These, and a few other pieces of evidence, indicate that dinosaurs may have been warm-blooded animals. However, we cannot be certain.

▲WHICH DINOSAURS HAD DUCK BILLS AND CRESTS?

The hadrosaurs, or duck-billed dinosaurs, appeared in the late Cretaceous period. Some of them had extraordinary crests on their heads.

The duck-billed dinosaurs were a group of plant-eating dinosaurs that evolved from the group known as ornithopods. They were the last and most specialized members of this group.

The long, flattened tails and ducklike beaks of these dinosaurs suggest that they lived in lakes or marshes. But the bill of a hadrosaur contained many tightly packed rows of crushing teeth that formed two grindstones. This suggests that they ate tough food. In fact there is evidence that they ate twigs and conifer needles. So hadrosaurs may have been forest feeders.

The purpose of the crests is unknown. They may have helped the animals' sense of smell. Or they may have acted as resonating chambers to increase the sound of the animals' calls.

Tanystropheus

Nothosaur

Placodont

▲WHEN DID THE FIRST SEA REPTILES APPEAR?

Reptiles are now basically land animals. Yet by the Permian period some had returned to live in water.

The first reptile to return to the sea was the Permian lizard-like animal *Mesosaurus*. It was over two feet long and had an eel-like tail and webbed feet for swimming.

During the Triassic period there were a number of sea reptiles. Placodonts were six-foor-long, heavily armored, newtlike animals that appear to have fed on shellfish. Nothosaurs were 10-foot-long amphibious reptiles with webbed feet and long necks. They were probably the ancestors of the later plesiosaurs.

One of the strangest of the early sea reptiles was *Tanystropheus*. This creature had a very long, stiff neck. It may have fed by standing in shallow water and reaching out and dipping its head in the water to catch squids and fish.

▼WHEN DID *IGUANODON* LIVE?

Iguanodon was an early Cretaceous dinosaur. It belonged to the group known as ornithopods, or bird-footed dinosaurs.

Ornithopods had existed since Triassic times. They were unspecialized, plant-eating dinosaurs that survived right through until the end of the Cretaceous period.

Iguanodon was a large ornithopod that grew to about 26 feet in length and stood over

16 feet tall. Its only real specialization seems to have been its thumb, which had become a sharp spike. This may have been used as a defensive weapon against large carnosaurs.

Ornithopods, like many modern plant-eating animals, may have lived in herds. The fossil remains of a herd of *Iguanodon* have been found in Belgium. Over 30 skeletons were found together. Perhaps the herd fell into a ravine while rushing away from an attacking predator.

▼WHEN DID ICHTHYOSAURS LIVE?

Ichthyosaurs appeared in the Triassic period and were a highly successful group until the middle of the Cretaceous period.

Ichthyosaurs looked amazingly like modern dolphins. They evolved almost exactly the same streamlined shape for high-speed swimming. An ichthyosaur swam by using its fishlike tail. A dorsal fin kept the reptile upright, and the flippers on each side were used

Elasmosaurus | Ichthyosaur | Short-necked plesiosaur

▲WHEN DID PLESIOSAURS LIVE?

Plesiosaurs were sea reptiles that appeared in the late Triassic period. They flourished until the end of the Cretaceous period.

There were two main types of plesiosaur. Long-necked plesiosaurs had small heads and needle-sharp teeth. They swam through the water in the same way as modern penguins. They used their paddles as "wings" and could twist and turn very rapidly. They fed

for steering and braking.

The first ichthyosaurs fed on fish, which they caught with their sharp teeth. Later types were able to tackle ammonites and squids. Some were almost toothless.

Ichthyosaurs could not move on dry land and so had to breed in water. Fossil evidence shows that they did not lay eggs. Instead they produced live young.

Ichthyosaurs began to die out during the early Cretaceous period. Possibly, they could not compete with the plesiosaurs.

mostly on fish. Some of the later long-necked plesiosaurs had very long necks indeed. *Elasmosaurus* had 70 neck bones and its neck made up half of its total length of 33 feet.

Short-necked plesiosaurs had much larger heads. They were strong swimmers and could move faster over long distances than their long-necked relatives. They fed mostly on squids and ammonites, which they caught in massive jaws. The largest short-necked plesiosaurs were over 40 feet long.

▶WHEN DID REPTILES
TAKE TO THE AIR?

Flying reptiles, or pterosaurs, first appeared in the Triassic period. They probably evolved from thecodonts that took to living in trees.

The ancestors of the pterosaurs were probably thecodonts that ran on their hind legs. Some took to scrambling about in trees, and some of these developed membranes for gliding. *Podopteryx* was a Triassic reptile that had membranes stretched between its front and hind limbs. It lived in trees and could glide from one to another.

One of the most primitive pterosaurs was a creature called *Dimorphodon*, which appeared in the early Jurassic period. It had a large head, and its jaws were armed with many large teeth. Its wingspan was about five feet, but it was probably a very poor flier. Like all pterosaurs, it probably used its wings for gliding rather than flying.

Rhamphorhynchus appeared in the last Jurassic period. Its head and body were much lighter than those of *Dimorphodon* and it was better adapted for life in the air. Its tail had a diamond-shaped structure on the end. This probably acted as a stabilizer when the reptile was in flight.

The forward-pointing teeth of *Rhamphorhynchus* may have been used for spearing fish. But it is unlikely that the animal could have dived into the water, or even landed on the surface. *Rhamphorhynchus* probably caught fish by skimming along the surface of the water and dipping its beak in.

Rhamphorhynchus

Pteranodon

Dimorphodon

▲WHICH WERE THE
BIGGEST FLYING
REPTILES?

The largest flying reptiles were pterodactyls such as *Pteranodon* and *Quetzalcoatlus*.

The pterodactyls were the most advanced group of pterosaurs. They had no tails, and their teeth were slender and delicate. Some had no teeth at all.

Pterodactylus was a small, sparrow-sized reptile. But *Pteranodon* and *Quetzalcoatlus*

were giants. Pteranodon had a wingspan of over 26 feet. It glided slowly over the sea, probably catching fish by scooping them up into its huge throat sac. *Quetzalcoatlus* was even larger, with a wingspan of about 33 feet. This enormous vulturelike reptile lived inland and probably lived on carrion.

Pterosaurs probably flapped their wings rather slowly and were amost certainly better gliders than fliers. On the ground they could hardly move. They probably lived on the tops of cliffs.

▼WHEN DID THE FIRST BIRDS APPEAR?

The earliest-known bird is *Archaeopteryx*, which lived in the late Jurassic period.

Birds probably evolved from thecodont or coelurosaur ancesters. Feathers probably evolved from reptile scales. Their first use would have been in helping to keep the animals warm.

Archaeopteryx was certainly a bird, as it had wings and feathers. But it also still had a number of reptilelike features.

Its beak contained sharp teeth, it had claws on its wings, and its long tail had bones down the middle.

Archaeopteryx is on its own in the fossil record. Nothing is known of its immediate ancestors or descendants. There is some evidence that there were a few gooselike and grebelike birds during the early Cretaceous period. Late Cretaceous birds were more widespread. They included *Ichthyornis*, a ternlike bird, and *Hesperornis*, a large, flightless diving bird.

Hesperornis

Archaeopteryx

Ichthyornis

▲COULD *ARCHAEOPTERYX* FLY?

Archaeopteryx does not seem to have been built for flying. It was probably better at gliding and may have spent most of its time on the ground.

In order to fly well, a bird needs a large breastbone to support the massive flight muscles. *Archaeopteryx* had a small, poorly developed breastbone.

Various suggestions have been made as to how *Archaeopteryx* lived. One idea is that it was a tree-dwelling creature that used its claws to scramble from branch to branch, and could glide from one tree to another. However, scrambling about in trees would soon have damaged its feathers.

Another idea is that *Archaeopteryx* lived on the ground and used its wings to catch prey. But it seems more likely that *Archaeopteryx* used its limited powers of flight to run and take off from high ground to escape from predatory coelurosaurs.

▼WHEN DID THE FIRST MAMMALS APPEAR?

The first mammals evolved in the Triassic period. They were tiny shrewlike creatures that lived on insects and other small animals.

Mammals evolved from a group called the cynodonts – one of the last groups of mammal-like reptiles. Mammals appeared during the Triassic period, at the same time as the dinosaurs were evolving. But, while the dinosaurs took over the world, the mammals remained a small and unimportant group.

During the Jurassic and Cretaceous periods several groups of mammals appeared. Their fossil remains consist mostly of teeth. The names of the groups describe the shapes of the teeth. Jurassic mammal groups included the docodonts, triconodonts and symmetrodonts. The most important group was the pantotheres. By the middle of the Cretaceous period, the pantotheres had given rise to the marsupials and placental mammals.

▼WHEN DID MAMMALS TAKE OVER FROM DINOSAURS?

The end of the Cretaceous period, 65 million years ago, marks the extinction of the dinosaurs.

The dinosaurs and a number of other animal groups appear to have died out as a result of dramatic changes in the world's climate. But we do not yet understand what caused these changes.

During the Paleocene epoch, the last of the Jurassic mammal groups died out. These were the rodentlike multituberculates, such as *Taeniolabis*, which had until this time been very successful. Meanwhile the placental mammals evolved rapidly. By the middle of the Eocene epoch there were 27 different groups. Insectivores and primates, such as *Plesiadapis*, were among the first to appear. There were also a number of "experimental" groups that quite soon became extinct. Among these were the amblypods, such as *Coryphodon*.

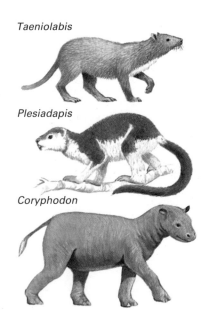

Taeniolabis

Plesiadapis

Coryphodon

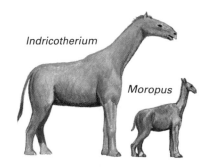

Indricotherium

Moropus

Brontotherium

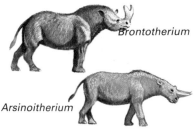

Arsinoitherium

▲WHEN DID GIANT MAMMALS ROAM THE EARTH?

The largest land mammal of all time was the giant hornless rhinoceros *Indricotherium*. It lived in the Oligocene epoch.

All the main animal groups have produced giant types, and the mammals are no exception. Some still exist today. The blue whale is still the largest animal that has ever lived.

Giant mammals were particularly common during the Oligocene epoch. The huge *Indricotherium* stood 18 feet high at the shoulder, and its head would have towered above a modern giraffe.

Brontotheres, such as *Megacerops* and *Brontotherium*, stood eight feet high or more at the shoulder. The horselike animal *Moropus* was only slightly smaller. All these animals probably grazed on the open plains. *Moropus* may have dug for roots.

Arsinoitherium was a strange two-horned animal, about the size of a modern rhinoceros. It lived in what is now Egypt and may have been a relative of the elephants and mastodons.

▼WHICH CATS HAD SABER TEETH?

Saber-toothed cats were probably the most formidable of the early mammal predators. They existed from the Eocene to the Pleistocene epoch.

The saber teeth of a saber-toothed cat are the greatly enlarged canine teeth of the upper jaw. They appear to have evolved as stabbing weapons for killing large tough-skinned prey. Saber-toothed cats had particularly powerful front limbs. This suggests that they held fast onto their prey while stabbing it to death.

Early saber-tooths, such as the Oligocene cat *Hoplophoneus*, had relatively short saber teeth. *Eusmilus* was a leopard-sized Oligocene cat with huge saber teeth. *Machairodes* was a lion-sized animal that was common in Europe during the Pliocene epoch. The most powerful of all the saber-tooths was *Smilodon*, which lived in North America. It died out at the same time as many of the large prey animals.

▼WHEN DID MASTODONS AND MAMMOTHS EXIST?

Mastodons first appeared in the Oligocene epoch. During the Pliocene epoch they gave rise to the elephants and mammoths.

The earliest mastodons, such as *Paleomastodon*, had short trunks and tusks and stood about six feet high at the shoulder. During the Miocene epoch there were three groups of mastodons. The deinotheres, or hoe-tuskers, had short, downward-pointing tusks. Short-jawed mastodons, like modern elephants, had long trunks and tusks. The American mastodon, *Mammut americanus*, lived in the tundra during the Pleistocene epoch.

Long-jawed mastodons formed the third group. One of the strangest types was the shovel-tusker, *Platybelodon*. It was from this group that the true elephants and mammoths evolved. The first known elephant is *Primelephas*, which lived in Africa during the Pliocene epoch. Mammoths also evolved in Africa, but the woolly mammoths lived in the tundra.

Platybelodon

American mastodon

Woolly mammoth

▼WHEN DID THE MODERN HORSE APPEAR?

The modern horse evolved about two million years ago, during the Pliocene epoch. Its ancestry can be traced back to a dog-sized animal called *Hyracotherium*.

Hyracotherium stood about 20 inches high at the shoulder. It had four toes on each front foot and it fed on soft woodland plants.

In North America the descendants of *Hyracotherium* were *Orohippus* and *Epihippus*.

The Oligocene horse *Mesohippus* had three-toed front feet and stood about two feet tall. All these horses were still woodland grazers, but the grasslands were now beginning to spread. *Parahippus* and *Merychippus* both had teeth that could grind up the tough grasses. Their descendants were all grazing horses. Some remained with three toes on each foot, but others lost the two outer toes. *Pliohippus* was the first of the one-toed horses and was the ancester of *Equus*, the modern horse.

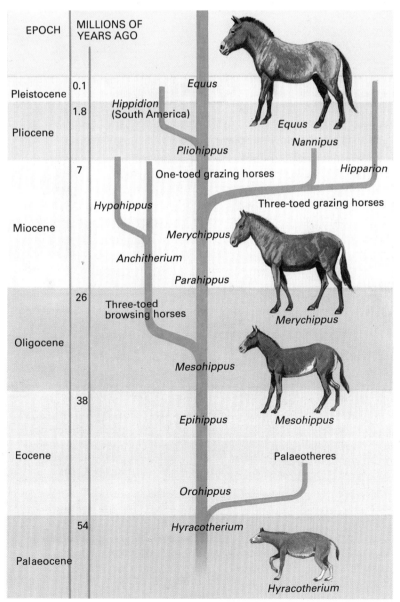

EPOCH	MILLIONS OF YEARS AGO		
Pleistocene	0.1	*Equus*	
Pliocene	1.8	*Hippidion* (South America)	*Equus*
		Pliohippus	*Nannipus*
	7	One-toed grazing horses	*Hipparion*
Miocene		*Hypohippus*	Three-toed grazing horses
		Merychippus	
		Anchitherium	
		Parahippus	
	26	Three-toed browsing horses	*Merychippus*
Oligocene		*Mesohippus*	
	38	*Epihippus*	*Mesohippus*
Eocene			Palaeotheres
		Orohippus	
	54	*Hyracotherium*	
Palaeocene			*Hyracotherium*

25

THE PAST

▶WHEN DID PEOPLE
FIRST MAKE TOOLS?

The first primitive people to use tools lived in Africa about 1.8 million years ago. Their fossil remains, and some of the tools they made, have been found at Olduvai Gorge in Tanzania.

The fossils were found by two paleontologists (people who study fossils), Louis and Mary Leakey. The Leakeys spent most of their lives exploring fossil sites in East Africa, where their son Richard still works.

The tools the early people used were made by taking pebbles and hammering away at one edge with a second rock until bits flaked off. Stones

flaked in this way have sharp edges, and they can then be used for cutting, scraping and chopping. These early people probably used the tools to kill animals and chop up the meat.

The Leakeys gave this early type of tool-user the scientific name *Homo habilis*, which means "handy man." *Homo habilis* walked upright, probably stood about four feet tall, and had a powerful grip.

▲WHEN DID THE
NEANDERTHALS LIVE?

Neanderthal people lived in Europe during the last Ice Age, which began about 70,000 years ago. Remains of Neanderthal people have also been found in the Middle East and North Africa.

The first remains were found in the Neander Valley, near Düsseldorf in West Germany, in 1856. Remains have since been found in other places, including Britain, France and Italy.

Neanderthal people were short and muscular, and not much over five feet tall. They had long, low skulls, with heavy ridges over the eyes. The Neanderthals lived in caves, and used fires to keep themselves warm.

Neanderthals made stone scrapers and hand-axes, and wooden spears. They hunted large animals such as the mammoth and the woolly rhinoceros. They buried their dead.

Neanderthals disappeared about 35,000 years ago.

were first found. They belonged to the same species as we do, *Homo sapiens sapiens* ("very wise man").

The Cro-Magnons lived in caves, and they made the splendid prehistoric cave paintings which have been found in France and Spain. The most important of these caves are at Lascaux in France and Altamira in Spain. The Cro-Magnons lived near the mouths of their caves, but they made their paintings deep inside.

The Cro-Magnons probably came to Europe from western Asia. They stood about five and a half feet tall, and their skeletons show that they were very like people of today.

The Cro-Magnons made better stone tools than the Neanderthals, but they seem to have been less suited than the Neanderthals to life in very cold climates. That is why they did not reach Europe during the worst of the Ice Age. But they were much cleverer than the Neanderthals.

▲ WHEN DID THE CRO-MAGNON PEOPLE LIVE?

Cro-Magnon people were one of the earliest known types of human being. The Cro-Magnons lived in Europe, Asia and North Africa from about 35,000 years ago.

The Cro-Magnons get their name from a cave at Les Eyzies, in southwestern France, where their bones

▶ WHEN DID PEOPLE FIRST SETTLE IN AMERICA?

The first people arrived in America some time between 28,000 B.C. and 23,000 B.C. They walked there from Asia across dry land where the Bering Strait now is.

During the Ice Age great sheets of ice covered the northern part of the world. So much water was frozen into this ice that the sea level fell. As a result, a lot of land that is now under the sea was dry.

The Bering Strait became dry on two occasions: between 28,000 B.C. and 23,000 B.C., and again between 14,000 B.C. and 10,000 B.C. Scientists

think that people crossed during each of these periods.

The first inhabitants of America, the American Indians, are Mongoloids – that is, they are similar in type to

the people of China, Japan and Siberia. The Indians of North America became farmers, or lived by gathering fruit and seeds or by hunting and fishing, as shown here.

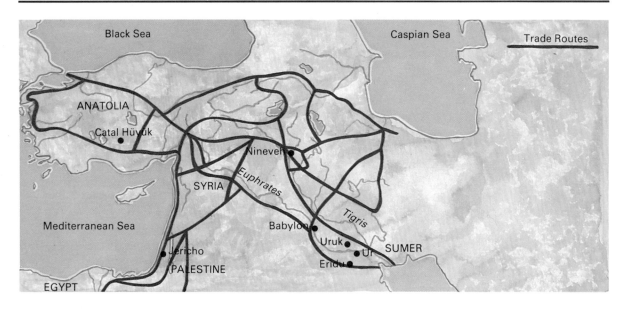

Map labels: Black Sea · Caspian Sea · Trade Routes · ANATOLIA · Catal Hüyük · Nineveh · SYRIA · Euphrates · Tigris · Mediterranean Sea · Babylon · Uruk · Ur · SUMER · Jericho · Eridu · PALESTINE · EGYPT

▲WHEN DID THE SUMERIANS LIVE?

Sumer was in the lower part of Mesopotamia, in what we now call Iraq. The Sumerians lived there before 3500 B.C., and held power until about 2000 B.C.

Nobody knows where the Sumerians came from, but it was probably either present-day Iran or Turkey. They were not Semitic like the other peoples of the region, such as the Assyrians and Hebrews. The Sumerians quickly built a number of cities. Among them were Eridu, Uruk, and Ur.

The earliest form of writing we know was found in the ruins of Uruk. It was drawn with pointed tools on clay tablets. At first the Sumerians wrote in pictograms, which are stylized drawings of objects. Later they began using simpler symbols which represented sounds. These later symbols were made with wedge-shaped pens, and they are called *cuneiform*, from a Greek word for "wedge."

The Sumerians were fine craftsmen, and many of their works of art have survived.

▲WHEN DID TRADE DEVELOP?

Trade began in Stone Age times, as soon as people had goods that they wished to exchange with one another.

Stone Age people probably traded food and animal skins. We do know that they traded the best-quality flints, for making their stone tools.

Trade increased as people became more civilized – that is, lived in towns and cities. The Sumerians living in Mesopotamia traveled along well-established routes all over the Middle East. One of the most important trading centers was Ur. The merchants there kept their accounts on clay tablets, many of which have survived.

The people of Ur manufactured goods such as cloth. They bartered them for valuable raw materials such as copper, gold and ivory. The goods went by sea to Dilmun, the ancient name for Bahrain. Other ships from further east brought copper and other materials to Dilmun from the Indus River, in Pakistan.

▲WHEN DID THE HEBREWS SETTLE IN PALESTINE?

According to the Bible, the Hebrews, led by Abraham, migrated to Palestine from the ancient city of Ur in Mesopotamia about 2000 B.C.

Scholars have not been able to confirm that Abraham actually came from Ur, though it is quite possible. But in 1975 archaeologists digging in Syria came across a startling find. It was a hoard of 15,000 clay tablets containing the official records of the lost city-state of Ebla. Ebla was one of the biggest cities of Syria in about 2000 B.C.

The tablets contain a number of names identical to those of people in the Bible, including Abraham, Esau and David. Even today, people tend to use the same personal names over hundreds of years, so the Hebrews may well have come from Ebla.

The Hebrews certainly seem to have spent some time in Egypt, and many scholars think they returned to Palestine in about 1260 B.C.

▼ WHEN WERE THE FIRST TOWNS BUILT?

The oldest town we know of was Jericho, which lies in the Israeli-held West Bank area of Jordan. It was first built about 12,000 years ago.

Stone Age hunters settled at Jericho around 10,000 B.C. and began to grow crops there. The original site of Jericho is a mound called Tell es-Sultan, just outside modern Jericho. It was an oasis on the edge of the desert. The people of Jericho built mud-brick houses and surrounded them with a huge stone wall, parts of which still survive.

Perhaps 3,000 people lived at Jericho. But a town twice its size has been discovered at Catal Hüyük, in southern Turkey. Çatal Hüyük was occupied for thousands of years from about 7100 B.C. Among the finds made in its ruins are the oldest known examples of pottery, textiles, mirrors, and walls covered with plaster and painted.

▲ WHEN WERE ANIMALS FIRST DOMESTICATED?

People began keeping animals instead of just hunting them before 8000 B.C. The first animals they kept were probably dogs, goats and sheep.

The dog was almost certainly the first animal to share its life with people. It may have domesticated itself, by looking for bones and scraps of food near camp fires. American Indians in Idaho had dogs by about 8400 B.C.

People in Iraq, Iran and other parts of the Middle East kept sheep and goats as food animals by around 7000 B.C. Pigs and cattle were domesticated soon after. Cattle were also used as draft animals, to carry loads and pull plows. The ass and the horse were also domesticated as draft animals by 3000 B.C.

In America and Australia there were no large animals that could be used as draft animals, except the llama of the Andes. Lack of animal-power there hampered the growth of civilizations.

▼ WHEN WERE LAWS FIRST WRITTEN DOWN?

The first laws to be written down were engraved on clay tablets during the reign of Urnammu, king of Ur from 2060 B.C. to 2043 B.C.

The tablets that have survived were obviously part of a *code*, or complete list of laws, but unfortunately we have only portions of it.

The earliest complete code of laws was compiled by King Hammurabi the Great, who ruled over Babylon from 1728 B.C. to 1686 B.C. Hammurabi had his laws engraved on a *stele*, an upright stone slab (shown here), which is now in the Louvre Museum in Paris.

The 282 laws cover disputes over land and other property, the fees payable for services, and family affairs. They also deal with crimes such as theft and assault. Nobody apparently went to prison, but the punishments were severe. Criminals were liable to be fined, to have their hands or ears cut off, or be put to death. A man who hit someone of higher rank was liable to be flogged.

▶ WHEN DID THE INDUS VALLEY CIVILIZATION FLOURISH?

The valley of the River Indus lies in Pakistan. One of the world's first civilizations grew up along its banks between 2500 B.C. and 1500 B.C.

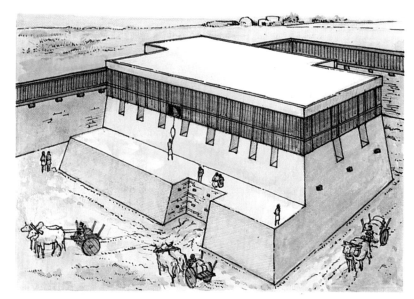

Like the other great early civilizations in Egypt, China and Mesopotamia, the Indus civilization grew up along a river, where there was plenty of water and good rich soil to grow crops.

There were about a hundred small towns and villages along the river bank, plus two large cities. One is called Mohenjo-Daro, a Hindu name meaning "mound of the dead." It lies about 280 miles upstream from Karachi. The other, further inland on a tributary of the Indus, is named Harappa.

The people of the Indus Valley built their cities of kiln-baked mud bricks. They laid out their streets on a grid pattern, and built brick sewers. Mohenjo-Daro had a fortified citadel, containing temples and a large granary (shown here). There was also a large public bath, possibly used for religious ceremonies.

The people of the Indus civilization had a system of weights and measures. They made objects of copper, bronze and silver, and used gold as jewelry. They were still halfway between the Stone Age and the age of metals, because they also used flint knives.

Objects made in ancient Babylonia have been found amid the ruins, showing that the Indus people engaged in long-distance trade.

Nobody knows how the Indus Valley Civilization ended. Flooding or invasion may have finished it.

▲ WHEN DID THE FIRST DYNASTIES RULE IN CHINA?

Dynasties are ruling families. The first of these families we know of was the Shang Dynasty. It governed China from about 1500 B.C. to 1027 B.C.

There may have been an even earlier dynasty, the Hsia. An ancient Chinese writer of history, Ssu-ma Ch'ien, referred to the Hsia, but no other traces of them have been found.

The Shang people built big cities in the flat plains near the Yellow River. Poor people lived in pits with thatched roofs over them. The richer people lived in large houses above ground. Tall earth banks surrounded the cities.

The nobles used chariots for hunting in peacetime and to take them into battle. In war each chariot carried two soldiers plus the driver.

The Shang made elaborate objects in bronze, and were also skilled sculptors. The Chou Dynasty overthrew the Shang in 1027 B.C.

▼WHEN WAS EGYPT RULED BY PHARAOHS?

The word *pharaoh* means "great house" or "royal palace." The Egyptians used the term for their kings from about 1570 B.C. until the Romans conquered Egypt in about 30 B.C.

For hundreds of years the Egyptians regarded their pharaohs not just as kings, but as gods, and supreme gods at that. An inscription to one pharaoh reads: "Adore the king . . . he is the One who creates all."

The pharaoh himself worshiped the sun god, Rê. Among his many titles was "Son of Rê." He was also called "King of Upper and Lower Egypt." Although in theory the pharaoh was all-powerful, in practice he had to abide by fixed rules.

The pharaoh is usually shown, in paintings and statues, wearing a double crown (for Upper and Lower Egypt). He carries a crook and a flail as emblems of his power. Queens are usually shown much smaller. Statues were always very stylized.

▼WHICH GODS DID THE EGYPTIANS WORSHIP?

The Egyptians had many gods. Some were local, worshiped in a particular region or city. Then there was Osiris, god of the dead, and people also worshiped the pharaoh and the sun.

The greatest local god was Amon, god of the air, who was worshiped in the city of Thebes. Amon later became identified with the sun god, Rê, as Amon-Rê.

Other local gods included the cat-headed goddess Bast; Apis the bull; and Thoth, the god of learning and the moon. Thoth was usually shown with the head of an ibis.

Osiris had the dual role of god of the dead and vegetation. His sister and wife, Isis, was regarded as "the mother of all things." Their son, Horus, was the god of Heaven. He is shown with a falcon's head. Setekh, the sky god, was the brother of Osiris. Anubis, shown as a jackal or with a jackal's head, was the god of death. The pharaoh was thought to personify Horus and Osiris.

▼WHEN DID PEOPLE FIRST WORK WITH METAL?

The oldest metal objects so far found were made of copper, before 7000 B.C. They were discovered at Çayönü Tepesi in Turkey.

These copper objects were made by hammering the metal cold. The makers used what is called "native" metal. This is metal occurring almost pure in small nuggets. Copper and gold are often found like this. The most important metal for early people was bronze. It is an alloy of copper and tin that is harder than either. The bronze stand shown here was made in Cyprus in the 1100s B.C.

Metal was not widely used until people discovered how to smelt it – that is, extract it from rock by heating it in a furnace. This probably happened about 4000 B.C. By the 3000s B.C. smiths in Mesopotamia (present-day Iraq) were making elaborate bronze objects. But they may not have been the first to do so. In Thailand, archaeologists have found a bronze spearhead dated at about 3600 B.C.

Osiris Anubis Thoth

▲ WHEN WAS CRETE THE HOME OF A GREAT CIVILIZATION?

The great civilization in Crete flourished between about 3000 B.C. and 1100 B.C. It is called the Minoan Civilization after its legendary king, Minos.

The civilization of Crete was forgotten for centuries. The only clue to it was a legend that every seven years the ancient Greeks had to send seven girls and seven young men as sacrifices to a terrible monster, the Minotaur, who lived in Crete.

In 1899 the archaeologist Arthur Evans found the remains of the Minoan civilization. He found that kings and nobles lived in large, luxurious palaces. Ordinary people lived in flat-roofed stone houses in small towns or villages.

The Minoans traded food in exchange for gold, silver, copper and other materials. They also made beautiful pottery.

◄ WHEN WAS THE PALACE OF KNOSSOS BUILT?

Work began on the Palace of Knossos in Crete about 2200 B.C. Most of what is standing today was built between 1775 B.C. and 1580 B.C.

The Palace at Knossos was one of several that have been found in Crete, and was probably the home of the Minoan kings. It was built on several floors around a central courtyard, and was full of large, airy rooms.

The walls of the main rooms were decorated with painted pictures. One is shown here. From these pictures we know that the wealthy people who lived in the palace wore fine clothes. Most of the women and men had curly black hair.

In 1450 B.C. a great disaster occurred which virtually ended the Minoan civilization. It was probably one of the many earthquakes which rock Crete from time to time and cause great destruction.

People from Mycenae, on the Greek mainland, lived on Crete for a time. In 1375 B.C. the Palace of Knossos was burned down.

► WHEN WAS STONEHENGE BUILT?

Stonehenge was built in three stages. The earliest was begun about 2750 B.C., and the last additions were made about 1300 B.C.

Nobody knows exactly what the purpose of Stonehenge was. It was undoubtedly a religious place, but it may also have been an observatory. Some of the stones are aligned with sunrise on Midsummer Day, and with moonrise on Midwinter Day.

Late Stone Age people

began Stonehenge by digging a huge circular ditch and bank. They also dug a ring of 56 pits, now called "Aubrey Holes" after the 16th-century writer John Aubrey, who found them.

Between 2000 and 1700 B.C., a long avenue was made between Stonehenge and the Avon River. Eighty bluestones, from Wales, were erected in a double circle. About 1700 B.C., huge blocks of sandstone capped by lintels were put up. More bluestones were erected about 1300 B.C.

►WHEN DID THE MYCENAEANS LIVE?

The Mycenaeans invaded Greece from Russia in about 2000 B.C. Their great city of Mycenae flourished from about 1450 B.C. to 1100 B.C., when it was destroyed by new invaders.

Mycenae was the home of King Agamemnon who, according to the poet Homer, led the attack on Troy. For years scholars thought Agamemnon and his people were legendary.

Then, in 1877, a group of royal tombs was found just inside the Lion Gate at Mycenae. The tombs were built 300 years before the time of Agamemnon. They were full of treasures made of gold, silver and alabaster.

The people of Mycenae dominated Greece for hundreds of years, sailing across the sea to Crete and other islands. They were engaged in almost constant warfare, and they built huge stone walls around their cities for defense. The picture shows the citadel at Mycenae.

▲WHEN DID THE TROJAN WAR TAKE PLACE?

The siege of Troy, which Homer described vividly in his poem the *Iliad*, took place somewhere about 1250 B.C.

Homer probably lived about 800 B.C., but practically nothing is known about him. His poem about Troy was based on older stories and legends, and is a mixture of fact and fancy. The poem is called the *Iliad*, from another name for Troy, Ilios.

According to Homer, Troy was besieged by a Greek army led by Agamemnon.

The ruins of Troy were rediscovered between 1870 and 1890 by a German, Heinrich Schliemann, who was fascinated by archaeology. We now know that Troy was destroyed and rebuilt many times. The earliest town on the site was probably built about 3000 B.C.

The Troy of the great siege was the seventh town to stand on the site. Its ruins show that it was plundered and set on fire.

▲WHEN DID THE PHOENICIAN TRADERS ROAM THE SEAS?

The Phoenicians were traders from about 2900 B.C. They were at the height of their power about 2,000 years later.

The Phoenicians lived in the coastal regions of what are now Syria, Lebanon and Israel. They were the Canaanites of the Old Testament of the Bible. Canaan and Phoenicia both mean "land of purple," and refer to the purple dye the Phoenicians made.

The Phoenicians were skilled craftsmen. They made glass and metalwork, carved in ivory and wood, and wove cloth. Their decorative furniture was famous. They also dealt in lumber, and in metal ores from Spain.

The Phoenicians set up several colonies, notably at Cadiz in Spain, and Carthage (near modern Tunis in Tunisia). Their bold sailors ventured into the Atlantic Ocean, and traded along the coast of West Africa and western Europe.

▼WHEN WAS THE PERSIAN EMPIRE FOUNDED?

The Persian Empire was founded by Cyrus the Great in 549 B.C. He extended his rule over most of western Asia.

Cyrus was king of Anshan, a small principality in south-western Iran. His overlord was Astyages, king of Media. Cyrus gradually got other Persian tribes on his side, and in 553 B.C. he began a rebellion against the Medes. By 549 B.C.

he had overthrown Astyages and became king.

Cyrus spent the next few years crushing opposition to his rule, and conquering the small principalities that acknowledged Media as their overlord. Cyrus called his new empire the Achaemenid Empire, after Achaemenes, an ancestor of his.

Cyrus then began a career of conquest. In turn he subdued Lydia in Asia Minor, all the lands that were dependent on Babylon, and finally Babylon itself. He was killed trying to conquer lands to the east.

▲WHEN DID DARIUS I RULE PERSIA?

Darius I seized the throne of Persia in 522 B.C., and ruled it until 486 B.C. He is often known as Darius the Great.

Darius was not the real heir to the throne of Persia, but the son of the governor of Parthia, a Persian province. When King Cambyses of Persia died in 522 B.C., civil war broke out, and the throne was taken by a man who claimed to be Cambyses' brother, Bardiya.

Darius and six Persian

noblemen killed Bardiya, and Darius made himself king. He claimed that "Bardiya" was really an imposter, but modern historians think Darius invented this story.

Darius was powerful. He soon brought his empire under control. He divided it into provinces, each ruled by a *satrap* (governor). To keep in touch with the provinces he had good roads made, along which royal messengers sped. Darius is shown here receiving tribute from his subjects.

▼WHEN DID THE BATTLE OF SALAMIS TAKE PLACE?

The Battle of Salamis was fought between a Greek fleet and a Persian fleet in 480 B.C. The Persians were heavily defeated.

For more than a hundred years the Persians tried to conquer Greece. Their first efforts failed, though they captured Cyprus and a number of Greek states in Asia Minor (modern Turkey).

In 480 B.C. King Xerxes of Persia began a new attack. He crossed the Hellespont (the old name for the Dardanelles) from Asia Minor into Europe, with a huge army. The army was supported by a large fleet.

Gradually the Persians drove the Greeks back, until they had to take up a defensive position on the Isthmus of Corinth. The Greek fleet sheltered in the nearby strait of Salamis. The Persian fleet attacked them there and was soundly beaten. A year later the Persian army was defeated at the Battle of Plataea, and the Persians were driven from Greece.

▼WHEN DID THE GREEK CITY-STATES ARISE?

The early Greeks began building fortified cities as long ago as 1500 B.C. These cities developed into different states because they lay in valleys that were separated by mountains.

The geography of Greece encouraged its people to be independent. Secure in its mountain-girt valley, each city developed its own way of life. People even spoke different dialects of Greek.

The earliest city-states were monarchies, but by about 600 B.C. most of the cities had got rid of their kings. Because they were small, the cities could settle major problems by a meeting of all the most important citizens. In this way, the idea of democracy (government by the people) gradually emerged.

The Greek city-states had to establish colonies if they wanted to expand. Colonies were set up in Italy, Sicily, Spain, southern France, and on the shores of the Black Sea.

In the 700s B.C. Sparta became the most powerful of the city-states. In the 400s the Greek cities banded together to fight off a Persian attack – the only time they ever united.

Soon afterward, Athens became the most important city. It had the finest writers, artists, sculptors and thinkers in all Greece.

Eventually Greece came under the domination of the northen state of Macedonia and its rulers Philip II and his son, Alexander the Great.

THE ACROPOLIS OF ATHENS

Parthenon

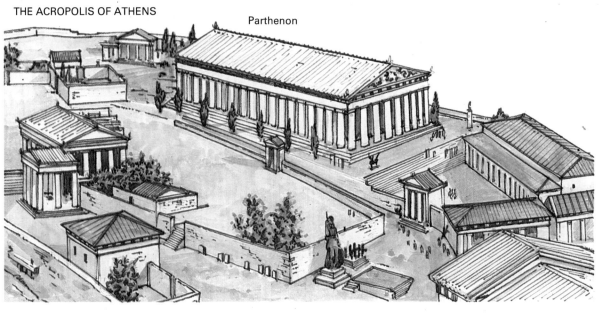

▲WHEN WAS THE GOLDEN AGE OF ATHENS?

Athens reached the height of its fame and influence during the rule of the statesman Pericles, from 461 to 431 B.C.

Pericles was a member of a noble Athenian family. He became the leader of a popular democratic party and, in effect, head of state in 461 B.C.

He was determined to make life better for the poor. When he came to power, poor people could not hold any of the offices of state because the posts were unpaid. Pericles introduced salaries for all public officials, and allowed the common people to hold any of the state posts.

Under his leadership the Athenians also began to rebuild their city, which had been partly destroyed during wars with Persia. Many of the buildings on the Acropolis, the hilltop citadel which dominates Athens, date from the city's "Golden Age." They include the Parthenon, a marble temple dedicated to the goddess Athena. It was decorated with sculptures by the great sculptor Phidias, the "Elgin Marbles".

Many great writers were active during the Golden Age. They included the playwrights Aeschylus and Sophocles, who wrote tragedies, and the comedy writer Aristophanes. The first great historian, Herodotus, lived in the Athenian colony of Thurii.

But Pericles also involved Athens in wars. In 404 B.C., after Pericles' death, Athens was defeated by Sparta.

▼ WHEN WAS ROME FOUNDED?

An old legend says Rome was founded in 753 B.C., but small settlements there probably existed earlier.

The legend, as told by the Roman writer Livy about 750 years later, says that Rome was founded by twins named Romulus and Remus. As babies, the twins were thrown into the Tiber River by a wicked uncle, but were rescued and suckled by a she-wolf. Later a shepherd found them and brought them up. Remus was killed, but Romulus became the first king of Rome.

This story seems to have been invented sometime in the 300s B.C. What probably happened was that several small tribes established settlements on the seven hills on which Rome is built. The first was probably on the Palatine, the most isolated of the hills.

Of the seven kings, the first four are almost certainly legendary, but the last three were probably real people – and foreign conquerors.

▼ WHEN DID ROME BECOME A REPUBLIC?

According to tradition the last king of Rome was deposed in 509 B.C. Elected consuls then ruled Rome.

The last king of Rome, Tarquin the Proud, was an Etruscan, from what is now Tuscany. The story goes that he was a tyrant, and his son, Sextus, was equally bad. Sextus tried to seize Lucretia, a married woman, and Lucretia killed herself. At this the Romans, led by Lucius Junius Brutus, rose in revolt and drove Tarquin from Rome.

Tarquin tried to regain power with the aid of another Etruscan king, Lars Porsena. But Horatius Cocles and two other Roman warriors delayed their army on a bridge over the Tiber River until the bridge could be demolished.

These stories are almost certainly legendary but it seems likely that the Romans did, about this time, drive out their Etruscan rulers. The picture shows Rome at the height of its power.

▼WHEN DID CAESAR CROSS THE RUBICON?

Julius Caesar was the greatest general of his time. He crossed the Rubicon River to invade Italy in 49 B.C.

Caesar ruled Rome with two other generals, Marcus Crassus and Gnaeus Pompeius (Pompey). This alliance is known as the First Triumvirate. Caesar went off to conquer Gaul (France), leaving the other generals in Rome.

Caesar was so successful that Pompey and Crassus became jealous of him. Crassus was killed in Mesopotamia (now in Iraq) and Pompey made himself dictator. He ordered Caesar to disband his army and return to Rome as a private citizen. This would have left Caesar defenseless and surrounded by enemies.

Caesar was also governor of a province north of Italy. He decided to act against Pompey. With 5,000 men he crossed the Rubicon, which separated his province from Rome. In two months he made himself master of Rome, and Pompey fled to Greece.

▼WHEN WAS ROME RULED BY EMPERORS?

The first emperor of Rome was Augustus, who came to power in 27 B.C. Emperors ruled Rome for more than 400 years.

Julius Caesar became the sole ruler of Rome in 49 B.C., but his rivals killed him in 44 B.C. Years of civil war followed.

The eventual victor was Caesar's great-nephew and heir, Gaius Octavius (Octavian). The members of the Senate, the ruling council of Rome, gave Octavian great powers and the title *Augustus*, which means "Majesty." Octavian was then known as Caesar Augustus. He also used the title *Imperator*. This originally meant "commander-in-chief," but in time it came to mean "emperor."

Augustus reorganized the government and the taxation system, set up a fire brigade and postal system, and made many new laws. His huge empire extended from Spain to Babylon, but his power and authority brought a long period of peace – the *Pax Romana*.

▼WHEN DID BARBARIAN TRIBES DOMINATE EUROPE?

Barbarian tribes moved south from northern Europe from the last century B.C. They overran most of Europe during the next 500 years.

Barbarian was a term used by the ancient Greeks, and later by the Romans, to describe people who they thought were less civilized than themselves. The barbarians probably came from Scandinavia. As their numbers increased, they moved southward in search of more land.

There were several barbarian tribes. The Jutes, Angles and Saxons invaded Britain. The Franks moved into what is now France, then called Gaul. The Burgundians took over northeastern Gaul, and the Vandals attacked Spain.

The Goths assaulted Italy and eventually took over Rome itself. There were two groups of Goths: the Ostrogoths, or "eastern Goths," and the Visigoths, or "valiant Goths." The Germanic tribes were in turn attacked by the Huns, nomads from central Asia.

▼ WHEN DID THE MAYA EMPIRE FLOURISH?

The Maya Empire was at its height in southern Mexico and Central America from about A.D. 250 to the 800s.

The Maya Indians developed a fine civilization in what are now Belize, Guatemala and southeastern Mexico.

The Maya built huge stone cities, had elaborate religious ceremoniesss, and developed a system off picture writing. They counted in twenties insteaad of tens as we do. Their priests were keen astronomers, and produced an accurate calendaar. The picture shows stonne slabs carved by the Maya.

The great Mayan cities were abandoned in the 800s. Nobody knows why. About a hundred years later another group, the Itza, set up a new civilization. This may have been an offshoot of the Maya, but was more likely connected with the Toltecs of central Mexico. The Toltecs in turn owed their civilization to an earlier group, the Olmecs. One of the last civilizations to develop was that of the Aztecs.

▼ WHEN WAS CHINA FIRST UNITED INTO ONE EMPIRE?

China's first empire was created by the Ch'in Dynasty (ruling family) in 221 B.C.

For 260 years the states of eastern China fought each other for control of the whole country. The struggle was eventually won by Ch'in, one of the westernmost states. Its leader was Prince Cheng, known as "the Tiger of Ch'in." When Ch'in won, Cheng proclaimed himself Shih Huang-ti, which means "the First Emperor."

Shih Huang-ti was an arrogant man, described as having "the mind of a tiger or a wolf." He set out to establish a strong central government. He standardized weights and measures, the written language, and even the width of carts, so that they could run easily on the deeply-rutted roads in all parts of the country.

Shih Huang-ti also ordered the building of the Great Wall of China to keep out invaders from the north.

▲ WHEN WAS THE HAN DYNASTY FOUNDED?

The Han Dynasty overthrew the Ch'in Dynasty in 202 B.C. It ruled China for more than 400 years.

The Ch'in emperor Shih Huang-ti made many enemies by his harsh rule and high taxes. As soon as he died, civil war broke out. His successor, called the "Second Emperor," was no match for the rebels.

The revolt was led by a petty official named Liu Pang and a man of gigantic strength, Hsiang Yu, who called himself "the Conqueror." They fell out, and Hsiang Yu was defeated by Liu Pang, who proclaimed himself emperor. The dynasty he founded is known as the Han, after Liu Pang's royal name, Han Kao-tsu.

During the Han Dynasty the Chinese empire expanded. Han scholars studied higher mathematics and astronomy. Paper was invented during this period, and Han traders visited Persia and Rome. The picture shows Han farmers at work in their fields.

▼WHEN DID THE FIRST INDIAN EMPIRE ARISE?

The first true empire in India was founded about 321 B.C. by Chandragupta Maurya. It is known as the Maurya Empire.

Chandragupta was commander-in-chief of the army of the Nanda Dynasty, who ruled over South Bihar in eastern India. He attempted a revolt that failed, then fled northwest to the Punjab, where he met the Greek conqueror Alexander the Great. After Alexander left India, Chandragupta received help from one of the Greek generals and soon became ruler of the Punjab and Bihar.

Within a few years Chandragupta's empire extended from the mouth of the Ganges River in the east to the mountains of the Hindu Kush, between modern Pakistan and Afghanistan. Chandragupta ruled over almost all of northern India and Pakistan. To keep order, he had a large army and an elaborate system of spies. A system of officials governed the empire.

STUPA AT SANCHI

▲WHICH INDIAN EMPEROR HELPED TO SPREAD BUDDHISM?

Asoka, the third of the Maurya emperors, spent much of his life helping to convert people to the religion of Buddhism.

Asoka was the grandson of Chandragupta Maurya. He became emperor in about 274 B.C.

For eight years Asoka waged wars and enlarged his empire. Then he became aware of the misery that war causes. He gave up the Hindu religion of his people to follow the teachings of the Buddha, who lived 250 years earlier.

Asoka ruled according to Buddhist ideals, especially those of nonviolence and friendliness. He had many Buddhist shrines, or stupas, built. Asoka also set up pillars which had his teachings carved on them. The lions shown in the picture formed the top of a pillar placed at Sarnath, where the Buddha preached his first sermon.

▼WHEN DID THE INCAS RULE IN SOUTH AMERICA?

The Inca civilization began to develop in Peru about A.D. 400, and reached its height in the 1400s.

The ancestors of the Incas lived among the mountains of Peru possibly as much as 4,000 years ago. The Incas began building up their country in about A.D. 1200.

From 1438 to 1493, two kings, Pachacuti and his son Topa Inca, expanded the Inca Empire. It eventually covered an area which extended northward into present-day Ecuador, and south into Bolivia, part of Chile and part of Argentina.

At its height, there were seven million people living in the Inca Empire. They were divided into nobles, common people and slaves.

The Incas' name comes from the title of their emperor (shown here), who was called the Inca. He ruled as a dictator through a system of governors.

The Inca people never invented writing, but used knotted cords called *quipu* to record numbers.

▼WHEN WAS THE BYZANTINE EMPIRE FOUNDED?

The Byzantine Empire was founded by the Emperor Constantine I in A.D. 330. It was an eastern division of the Roman Empire.

The Roman Empire was divided in two by the Emperor Diocletian in 286. By the time Constantine came to the throne, the eastern part of the empire was more important than the western part.

Constantine decided to move the headquarters of the empire to the east. He built a new city as his capital, which he called Constantinople after himself. It is now Istanbul.

Constantinople was built on the site of a small town named Byzantium. The term "Byzantine Empire" is one used by modern historians. Its people always thought of themselves as Romans.

The Byzantine Empire lasted until 1453, when Constantinople was captured by the Ottoman Turks. The picture shows a mosaic of Constantine IX, who ruled from 1042 to 1055.

▼WHEN DID ISLAM BECOME A MAJOR RELIGION?

Islam was founded by the prophet Muhammad, in Arabia. It spread rapidly in the years immediately after his death in A.D. 632.

The word Islam means "submission," and implies the obedience of its followers to the will of God. They are called Muslims, which means "those who submit."

The basis of Islam is the *Koran*, a holy book. Muslims believe that the Koran contains the words of God, revealed to Muhammad by the archangel Gabriel in a series of visions.

Muslims do not worship Muhammad, but regard him as the last in a series of major prophets which include the Old Testament prophets and Jesus.

Muhammad did not write down the words of the *Koran*. They were written down by his followers as he taught them, and took its final form about 652, during the reign of the caliph Othman.

▲WHEN DID THE ISLAMIC EMPIRE FLOURISH?

The Islamic Empire lasted from A.D. 632 to 1256. It stretched from Spain to India.

After Muhammad died in 632, his friend and chief adviser Abu Bakr was elected caliph. Caliph means "successor." From then on, the Islamic Empire was ruled by caliphs.

Abu Bakr and his successors launched a *jihad* (holy war) to convert people to the Muslim faith. Within 12 years of Muhammad's death, the caliph controlled Arabia, the whole of the Middle East, including part of Persia, and all of Egypt.

By 750, Islam had spread along the North African coast. The Moors, Muslims from Morocco, had also conquered most of Spain and Portugal. The Muslims also reached western India and central Asia.

Trade and learning flourished in the Islamic Empire. Muslim merchants traveled far and wide to trade in luxuries such as silks and spices.

▼ WHEN WERE THE MONGOL TRIBES UNITED?

The wild Mongol tribes of the Asian plains were united in 1206 by a chieftain named Temujin, later called Genghis Khan.

The Mongols were nomads who wandered over the bleak countryside with their herds of horses and cattle. They lived in felt tents called *yurts*, and were skilled hunters and fierce warriors.

Temujin was born in 1162. He was a very strong man, and was a born leader. He was loyal to his friends but he punished traitors severely.

In his early years, Temujin survived many attempts to kill him by rival tribes. The Merkits were a tribe from the frozen lands further north. On one occasion, they captured Temujin's wife, Bourtai, in a night raid. But with the aid of another tribe, the Karaïts, he won her back.

Soon after, Temujin led his Mongols to victory against an attack by twice their number of Taidjuts. By this and other victories he gradually gained the respect of other tribes. More and more people came under his rule.

When he was about 40 years old, Temujin was proclaimed *Genghis Khan*, which means "King of the Oceans." In 1206 he was elected as Great Khan, ruler of all the Mongol peoples. He set up a code of laws, and began to train his unruly warriors into a disciplined force. Once this army was formed, Genghis Khan set out to conquer other lands.

▲ WHEN DID THE MONGOLS RULE ASIA?

The Mongol Empire reached its greatest extent by 1294, when it stretched from the Danube River in the west to the Pacific Ocean in the east.

Genghis Khan began his conquests with an attack on China. At first his warriors were trained only for open warfare on the plains. They had no siege engines to attack fortified towns. But they soon captured skilled Chinese soldiers and made them help.

Genghis Khan also practiced "psychological warfare." He terrorized people into surrender with horrific tales of what would happen if they resisted the Mongols.

The Mongols broke their way through the Great Wall Of China in 1213. By 1215 Peking had surrendered, and Genghis Khan ruled over north China. He then set out for the west, and in a six-year campaign swept through Persia and Afghanistan into southern Russia.

When Genghis Khan died, his empire was divided among his four sons. One of them, Ogotai, led an army of 150,000 horsemen into Hungary and Poland in a devastating raid.

The empire was reunited later when Genghis's grandson, Kublai Khan, was elected Great Khan in 1260. He still had rivals, including his own younger brother, but he defeated them all. Kublai completed the conquest of China. He founded a new dynasty, the Yüan, which ruled China until 1368. After Kublai died, in 1294, the Mongol Empire broke up.

▼WHEN DID VIKINGS COLONIZE EUROPE?

Vikings raided European lands and founded colonies for about 200 years up to around A.D. 1000.

The Vikings were pirates from Scandinavia. They were bold and skillful navigators, who sailed the European seas in their long, elegant ships. Each ship had a large, square sail, but could also be driven by oars.

At first the Vikings went in search of plunder. They often raided monasteries, where some of the greatest wealth could be found.

From 793 onward, Vikings from Norway raided England. They began to settle there in the late 800s. Other Vikings started settlements in the Orkneys, Shetlands and Hebrides. Settlers sailed in shorter, wider ships, as shown in the picture.

Vikings attacked France and settled there. They were known as Northmen, or Normans, and gave their name to Normandy. Others reached Spain, Sicily, Italy and Russia.

▲WHEN DID THE VIKINGS REACH AMERICA?

America was probably first sighted in about 986 by a Viking named Bjarni Herjólfsson, but the first visit was by Leif the Lucky in A.D. 1000.

Vikings settled in Iceland about 870. Among them was a warrior named Eric the Red, so called for his habit of feuding and killing. Eric was exiled from Iceland for three years. He founded a settlement further west, now Greenland.

Bjarni Herjólfsson was on his way to Greenland from Iceland when he was blown off course and sighted land to the west. Eric's son, Leif Ericsson (known as Leif the Lucky) heard Bjarni's story. He decided to make a voyage to the west himself.

Leif reached the coast of Labrador and cruised south until he came to a land where wild grapes grew. He called it Vinland. Vikings later tried to settle there, but were driven away by hostile Indians.

▼WHEN WAS EUROPE GOVERNED UNDER THE FEUDAL SYSTEM?

The feudal system existed in Europe during the Middle Ages, from about A.D. 700 to the 1400s.

The term "feudal system" is used by historians to describe a system under which a person held land in return for military or other service. The land was called a *fief*, or *feodum* in medieval Latin.

The feudal system began in the kingdom of the Franks (now France) and spread gradually over western Europe. It reached its height in the period from the 800s to the 1200s, but disappeared in the 1400s.

In its simplest form, the feudal system could be seen as a pyramid. At the top was the king. He let the great barons have lands in return for providing him with soldiers when he needed them. The barons in turn gave land to lesser lords or knights in return for their services. Peasants also held land from each lord in return for working on his land.

▼WHEN WERE MONASTERIES FOUNDED IN EUROPE?

The first monasteries in Europe were founded in Italy and France in the A.D. 300s.

The earliest Christian monastery was founded by St. Anthony of Egypt in the Egyptian desert in the early 300s. St. Anthony himself spent most of his life as a hermit, in a cave.

Christians in Italy and Gaul (as France was then called) were inspired by St. Anthony's example. St. Martin, bishop of Tours, established an important monastery at nearby Marmoutier. From there, monks traveled to take the monastic idea to many lands.

An important step was taken by St. Benedict of Norcia in Italy. In 529 he established a monastery at Monte Cassino, which still flourishes. There he wrote his *Rule*, a code of conduct for monks which has been followed ever since. Monasteries became the main centers of learning in Europe during the Middle Ages.

▼WHEN WAS JAPAN RULED BY SHOGUNS?

The first shogun to rule Japan was Minamoto Yoritomo in 1192. The last shogun resigned in 1867.

The word *shogun* means commander-in-chief. It was originally used in the 700s as a purely military title. Japan was then, as now, ruled by an emperor, but real power was in the hands of the Fujiwara family, who acted as regents.

In 1160 the Taira family seized power from the Fujiwaras, only to be defeated by the Minamoto family led by Yoritomo. From then on the shoguns acted as military governors of Japan.

The title of shogun became hereditary. It was held by the Minamoto family until 1336, when the Ashikaga family took over. They ruled until 1573. The Tokugawa family took over in 1603. In 1867 several important *daimyo* (noblemen) banded together to overthrow the shogun. The emperor then took over the shogun's powers.

▲WHEN WERE GREAT CASTLES BUILT IN JAPAN?

The great period of castle-building in Japan was in the 1500s and 1600s. At that time the country was divided into many small states at war with one another.

Every local chief had a heavily fortified home. Warriors known as samurai fought on horseback for their lords. But castle-building really developed when a warrior named Toyotome Hideyoshi became shogun in 1585.

Hideyoshi built a series of castles to help him control Japan. Each castle consisted of a palace surrounded by defensive walls, lookout towers and a moat. Japanese castles were similar to the medieval castles of Europe, but their central buildings were not so heavily built as the keeps of European castles.

Hideyoshi's successor as shogun was Tokugawa Ieyasu. He ended the long period of civil war that had ravaged Japan, and castles ceased to be of military importance.

▶ WHEN DID THE SWISS BECOME INDEPENDENT?

The Swiss gained their independence from the Holy Roman Empire in 1499. This was officially accepted by the Empire in 1648.

In the early Middle Ages Switzerland consisted of several cantons, or states, which formed part of the Holy Roman Empire.

Three cantons – Uri, Schwyz and Unterwalden – formed a league in 1291, but did not then claim independence. They took the name Switzerland from Schwyz. Other cantons joined them later.

Between 1315 and 1388, the Swiss defeated three attempts by Austria to subdue them. One of their earliest victories was the Battle of Margarten in 1315, shown here.

In 1499 the Swiss defeated the army of Maximilian I, the ruler of the Holy Roman Empire, and became independent. After a defeat by the French in 1515, Switzerland became a neutral country and has stayed so ever since.

◀ WHEN WAS JOAN OF ARC BURNED AT THE STAKE?

Joan of Arc freed much of France during the Hundred Years' War. She was burned to death for heresy by the English in 1431.

Joan was a peasant girl. Her name in French is Jeanne d'Arc. She was born at Domrémy, in eastern France, in 1412. When she was 17, Joan heard voices which she said commanded her to free her country from the English, who controlled the northern half of France.

Joan went to the young king of France, Charles VII, who had not even been crowned, and demanded to lead his army. Charles agreed. Wearing armor and a sword, Joan led French forces to save the town of Orléans, which was under siege by the English. She won four other battles and saw Charles crowned at Rheims.

In 1430 Joan was captured by troops of Burgundy, who sold her to their allies, the English. They put her to death.

▶ WHEN DID THE BLACK DEATH SWEEP ACROSS THE WORLD?

The Black Death was an outbreak of bubonic plague. It ravaged Asia and Europe between 1334 and 1351.

Bubonic plague is named after the buboes, or swellings, that appear on the bodies of its victims. It has been known at least since the days of the Romans, and possibly existed in Biblical times.

The epidemic of plague known as the Black Death started in central Asia. It was carried by fleas that lived on rats. Ships and overland trading caravans carried the plague westward. By 1346 it had reached the Crimea. From there it was carried to Europe by ships.

The plague reached Europe in 1348. By the end of 1350 it had swept through most of Europe. The outbreak was over by the end of 1351. About one person in three died from the plague during this time. Bodies were carted away for burial by corpse-collectors.

▶ WHEN DID THE ITALIAN CITY-STATES ARISE?

The Italian city-states began to develop in the 1000s. They became independent in the late Middle Ages. Some became rich and powerful.

After the fall of the Roman Empire in 476 there was no strong central government in Italy. Lombards from Germany occupied the north. Normans from Normandy set up a kingdom in the south which included Sicily. The popes controlled the Papal States in central Italy.

From the late 900s, northern Italy became part of the Holy Roman Empire. Because the emperor lived far away in Germany, some of the cities began to gain independence.

Coastal cities with the best opportunities for trade grew rich and powerful first. Among them were Pisa, Genoa and Venice. Other important cities included Milan and Florence. Some cities were ruled by dictators, but they were often controlled by assemblies of citizens, especially the rich merchants.

▲ WHEN DID VENICE BECOME RICH?

Venice began to grow rich in the 800s. It reached the height of its wealth and power in the 1400s.

Venice (shown here) is built on a group of islands in the Adriatic Sea, off the coast of Italy. Fishermen and traders fled there in the 400s to escape from the barbarians who were raiding Italy. By the 800s they had built Venice, and were trading by sea with Constantinople and other Mediterranean cities.

Venice was ruled by a leader called a *doge*, who was elected from among the most powerful families. From 1310 onward, however, real power was held by a group called the Council of Ten.

By the 1400s Venice controlled trade in the eastern Mediterranean. Silks and spices from the East were imported into Europe in Venetian ships. Great churches and palaces were built along the canals of Venice by rich merchants.

◀ WHEN WAS THE HANSEATIC LEAGUE FORMED?

The Hanseatic League was an association of German towns. They banded together for trade and protection in the late 1200s.

"Hanseatic" comes from an old French word, *hanse*, meaning a guild. At its height, the Hanseatic League was like a small-scale Common Market. Merchants in a number of north German towns formed a series of *hanses* for trading abroad, particularly with England and Flanders (modern Belgium).

The merchants of Hamburg and Lübeck cooperated first. They made an agreement to combat robbery in the area. They soon found that working together made them stronger than their competitors when trading in the Baltic Sea area. Almost all the larger cities on the shores of the Baltic and North seas eventually joined the League. The picture shows Hanseatic merchants discussing trade.

▼ WHEN WAS THE OTTOMAN EMPIRE FOUNDED?

The Ottoman Empire was founded by the Turkish sultan Osman, who died in 1326. The Ottoman Turks take their name from him.

The Ottoman Turks came from Asia Minor, which is now known as Turkey. Until 1071, Asia Minor was part of the Byzantine Empire. Then it was conquered by Seljuk Turks.

Shortly before 1300, the Ottoman Turks began to build their empire. They were based at first in Bithynia, in the north of Asia Minor. Soon they had conquered almost all of Asia Minor. In 1345 they crossed into Europe, and by 1400 they controlled most of the Balkan peninsula, from Bulgaria to Greece.

The Ottoman Empire grew fast. Its lands stretched from North Africa to the Middle East. The Ottoman army even laid siege to Vienna, but failed to capture it. At first, the huge empire was strong, but gradually it lost much of its power.

▼ WHEN WAS THE LAST MAJOR BATTLE WITH GALLEYS FOUGHT?

The last major battle with galleys was the Battle of Lepanto. It was fought near Greece on October 7, 1571, between a Christian fleet and a Muslim Turkish force.

In 1570 the city of Venice appealed for help to the pope and Spain against the Turks who were attacking the Venetian colony in Cyprus.

After much argument, a Christian fleet was assembled to fight the Turks. It consisted of ships from Venice, Spain, Malta, Genoa and Savoy.

The main ships in both the Christian and Turkish fleets were galleys. These were long, slim warships driven by oars. They were easier to maneuver than sailing ships.

The Turkish fleet consisted of 274 galleys carrying 88,000 men. The Christian fleet had 316 galleys, including small craft, and 80,000 men. It was commanded by Don Juan of Austria. The battle lasted five hours before the Christian fleet won.

▲ WHEN DID THE OTTOMAN TURKS CAPTURE CONSTANTINOPLE?

Constantinople was the capital of the Byzantine Empire. The Ottoman Turks captured it in 1453.

By 1400 the Ottoman Turks had overrun all the Byzantine lands except a small area around Constantinople. The Byzantine emperor had to acknowledge the Turkish sultan as his overlord.

From 1424 onward, Sultan Murad II was content to live at peace with the emperor. But when the sultan died in 1451 he was succeeded by Muhammad II, whose ambition was to conquer Constantinople.

Muhammad built a castle, now called Rumili Hisar, on the European shore of the Bosporus near Constantinople. With this as a base, he began to besiege the city in March 1453. The final assault (shown here) began on May 25. In a few hours the Turks captured Constantinople. They renamed it Istanbul.

▼WHEN DID THE RENAISSANCE BEGIN?

The Renaissance was a revival of learning and a change in people's ways of thinking. It began in Italy around 1300, and lasted about 300 years.

The word *Renaissance* means "rebirth." It was first used in the 1800s to describe this great period of change.

The Renaissance began in the Italian city of Florence (shown in the picture). One of its pioneers was the painter Giotto. Unlike other artists of his time, he painted figures that looked realistic.

Writers, led by the poet Petrarch, began to explore the almost forgotten literature of ancient Greece and Rome. Their own writings were influenced by these works.

Architects such as Filippo Brunelleschi studied Greek and Roman buildings and began to design new buildings in a similar style.

The Renaissance received an enormous boost from the invention of printing. This was the work of a German goldsmith, Johannes Gutenberg of Mainz, around 1440. Before printing was invented, books were rare objects because they were copied slowly and laboriously by hand. Now more people could study new ideas.

The Renaissance spread from Italy to France in the late 1400s, and soon reached Germany, the Netherlands and Britain. It reached its peak in the 1500s, a period known as the High Renaissance. An offshoot of the Renaissance was the Reformation, the great change in religion.

▲WHEN DID THE MEDICIS RULE FLORENCE?

Members of the Medici family were involved in politics in Florence from the early 1200s, but their real power began in 1434. It lasted until 1737.

The power and influence of the Medicis came from their great wealth. They were bankers involved in international dealings. Giovanni dé Medici (1360-1429) was probably the richest man in Italy.

Giovanni's son Cosimo rose to supreme power in 1434. Cosimo never held office, but he influenced all the decisions of the city council. Florentines later called him "the father of his country." Cosimo spent large sums of money on the arts, and many of the famous Renaissance artists were supported by him.

The greatest of the Medicis was Cosimo's grandson Lorenzo (1449-1492), known as "the Magnificent." Under his rule, Florence (seen here) became the most powerful city-state in Italy. Architects and artists worked to make it also one of the most beautiful. After Lorenzo died, the Medici had some weak rulers. The family was twice exiled and twice restored.

Three of the Medicis became pope. They included Leo X, Lorenzo's son, and Clement VII, his nephew. The third, Leo XI, was elected pope in 1605, but died 27 days later.

Two Medicis became queens of France. Catherine married Henry II, and Marie married Henry IV. Their name in France was spelled *de Médicis*.

Henry VIII and Anne Boleyn

◄WHEN DID THE ANGLICAN CHURCH BREAK WITH ROME?

The break between the Church in England and the Pope came with the Act of Supremacy of 1534. This named Henry VIII and his successors as Supreme Head of the Church of England.

At first the Reformation in England was not a matter of beliefs but was dictated by political reasons. The basic cause was that Henry VIII had no male heir, and his wife, Catherine of Aragon, was too old to have another child. Henry asked the Pope to annul (end) the marriage so that he could marry a younger woman, Anne Boleyn.

The Pope refused to annul the marriage. Henry felt he had no alternative but to break with Rome and have an English court grant him a divorce. This political move led to religious changes. The English, or Anglican, Church became quite separate from the Roman Catholic Church. Henry also abolished the monasteries in England.

▲WHEN WAS THE SOCIETY OF JESUS FOUNDED?

The Society of Jesus was founded by St. Ignatius Loyola in 1534.

Loyola (shown here) was a Spanish soldier who became a priest. He and six other men formed this Roman Catholic society in Paris. It was approved by Pope Paul III in 1540.

Its members, called Jesuits, have a special interest in education and missionary work.

▲WHEN WAS THE MASSACRE OF ST. BARTHOLOMEW'S DAY?

The massacre took place on August 24, 1572, in Paris. It spread to other cities during the next few days.

The cause of the massacre was the enmity between the Roman Catholics in France and the Protestants, known as Huguenots. A civil war between them lasted from 1562 to 1570.

Several Huguenots held high office, and many Catholics feared that they would gain too much power. Among those who feared the Huguenots most was Queen Catherine dé Médicis. She was the mother of Charles IX.

In August 1572, Huguenots flocked to Paris for the wedding of one of their leaders, Henry, King of Navarre, to Catherine's daughter, Margaret. Urged by Catherine, Charles ordered the assassination of the leading Huguenots. Armed mobs began the slaughter early in the morning of St. Bartholomew's Day; 5,000 people were killed.

▼ WHEN WAS RUSSIA FIRST UNITED?

Russia was united by Ivan III, Grand Prince of Moscow, who reigned from 1462 to 1505.

Moscow was one of several Russian states when Ivan became grand prince in 1462. They included Lithuania, Novgorod and Pskov. To the south and east lay three Mongol states: the Crimea, Kazan and the territory of the Golden Horde.

The Golden Horde claimed overlordship over Moscow and demanded a yearly tribute. When Ivan refused to pay, the Mongols marched to attack.

Ivan faced up to the threatened onslaught. His brothers, Boris and Andrei, supported him with 20,000 men, and the Mongols retreated.

Soon afterward, the Mongols fell out among themselves and Moscow was safe from attack. Ivan also won control of Novgorod and Pskov, thus uniting Russia. He adopted the title of *tsar*, which means "Caesar."

▲ WHEN WAS INDIA RULED BY THE MOGULS?

The Mogul Empire was founded in 1526 by Babur, the ruler of Kabul in Afghanistan.

Mogul is an Indian equivalent of "Mongol." Babur was part Mongol by birth. He is shown here with his courtiers in a garden.

Several Afghan tribes were quarreling over the right to rule Delhi when Babur decided to intervene. He won a decisive victory at Panipat, and made himself master of Delhi and its territory.

Babur's grandson, Akbar, ruled from 1556 to 1605. He extended the Mogul Empire throughout northern India as far as Kashmir. It reached its greatest size during the reign of Aurangzeb (1658-1707). It then included almost all of present-day India, Pakistan and Bangladesh.

After that the empire slowly declined as the British gained control. The last Mogul emperor lost power in 1858, after the Indian Mutiny.

Ivan III

Ivan IV

▲ WHEN DID IVAN THE TERRIBLE RULE RUSSIA?

Ivan IV was the grandson of Ivan III. He ruled from 1533 to 1584. His brutality gave him the nickname of "the Terrible."

Ivan IV came to the throne at the age of three, but did not begin to rule for himself until 1547, when he was almost 17. For several years his cruelty was kept in check by his wife, but she died in 1560.

While Ivan was a boy, Russia was ruled by a council of *boyars*, the rich noblemen. Ivan decided to curb the power of the boyars and so began a reign of terror. He could not forgive the bad way in which the boyars had treated him.

Ivan formed a bodyguard of secret police, called the *oprichniki*. At his command, the oprichniki hunted down and killed all the boyars whom he suspected of treason. In 12 years more than a thousand boyars were killed. Ivan grew more mad as he grew older, and even killed his eldest son in a quarrel.

▶WHEN WERE THE EAST INDIA COMPANIES FOUNDED?

The East India companies were trading organizations founded in the 1600s by European countries. The English, French and Dutch companies were the most important.

Other East India companies were established by Austria, Denmark, Scotland, Spain and Sweden. Few of these lasted long, but the Danish company sold out to the English company as late as 1845.

The Portuguese discovered the sea route to India in 1497-1499, and at first they had a monopoly of trade with India. The Dutch soon gained control of the islands that now form Indonesia, which were a rich source of spices.

The English East India Company was formed in 1600, the Dutch company in 1616, and the French company in 1664. France and England competed for trading and military control of India during the 1700s. Between 1750 and 1763 France and Britain fought each other in India. From 1756 they fought in Europe too, in the Seven Years' War. After the French were defeated, they kept only a few bases in India.

The British soldiers in India were in the service of the East India Company. They were commanded by one of the company's officials, Robert Clive. The Mogul emperor, seen in the picture with Clive, lost much of his power to the British.

The East India Company ruled India until the Indian Mutiny of 1857. After that the British government ruled India directly.

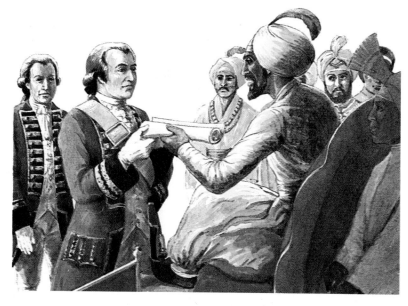

▼WHEN DID THE THIRTY YEARS' WAR TAKE PLACE?

The Thirty Years' War raged in Europe from 1618 to 1648. It began as a religious civil war in Germany and ended by involving most European countries.

The war began as a dispute over whether a Roman Catholic prince or a Protestant one should be king of Bohemia; and also whether a Catholic should be elected as Holy Roman Emperor.

The Catholic contender, Ferdinand, became both king of Bohemia and emperor. The Danish king, Christian IV, then fought on the Protestant side but he was defeated in 1629.

The Swedish king, Gustavus Adolphus, then entered the war, also on the Protestant side. He was supported by France, whose chief minister was the Roman Catholic Cardinal Richelieu.

By the time peace was made, in 1648, Germany had been devastated and millions of innocent people had been killed.

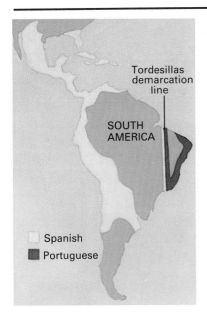

▲ WHEN DID A POPE DIVIDE UP THE WORLD?

▲ WHEN DID THE AZTECS THINK THAT GOD HAD ARRIVED ON EARTH?

▲ WHEN DID 180 MEN CONQUER AN EMPIRE?

Pope Alexander VI made the division in 1493 to prevent disputes between Spain and Portugal.

Christopher Columbus reached the West Indies in 1492. He thought that he had arrived in the outer islands of Japan, and reported this to his masters, the Spanish rulers Isabella and Ferdinand.

Ferdinand and Isabella knew that the Portuguese were already trying to reach the riches of the East by sailing eastward around Africa. They appealed to Pope Alexander VI for a ruling that would divide the "unknown" world fairly between Spain and Portugal.

The pope drew an imaginary line from pole to pole, 100 leagues (345 miles) west of the Azores. He gave Spain rights to the west of it and Portugal rights to the east. In return, the Spanish and Portuguese had to convert the people of their new lands to Christianity. The line was later moved further west by the Treaty of Tordesillas between Spain and Portugal.

When Hernan Cortés landed in Mexico in 1519, the Aztecs thought he was their god Quetzalcoatl.

The Aztecs had a legend that Quetzalcoatl, the Feathered Serpent, had come to earth in human form. He had a black beard and white skin. After a time he sailed away to the east. Prophets said he would come back one day, dressed in black.

Cortés lived in the Spanish colony of Cuba. Although rich, he was anxious to explore the lands that lay further west. Cortés sailed to Mexico with 11 ships and a few hundred men. He was white-faced, black-bearded, and wore black clothes. He also arrived in what the Aztec calendar called a "One-Reed Year" – just the time that Quetzalcoatl was expected.

The Aztecs were terrified of the guns and horses that Cortés brought with him. Within two years Cortés had conquered the Aztecs and all of Mexico.

Francisco Pizarro was a Spanish soldier. He conquered the Inca Empire of Peru in 1532, with only 180 men.

Pizarro and a fellow soldier, Diego de Almagro, had already found the Peruvian empire six years earlier. They realized it was rich in gold and were determined to capture it.

Pizarro sailed from Panama in 1531 with three ships. His tiny force included his three brothers. Pizarro found the Inca Empire in a state of civil war. The emperor, Atahualpa, had been fighting his brother, Huascar, and had just captured him.

Pizarro captured Atahualpa by treachery. He asked for an enormous ransom of gold and silver which the emperor paid. While in custody, Atahualpa gave orders for his brother to be killed. Almagro and another 150 men arrived to support Pizarro. The two Spaniards accused Atahualpa of treachery, and had him strangled. Soon they were masters of Peru.

▼WHICH FRENCH RULER WAS KNOWN AS THE "SUN KING?"

Louis XIV was known as the "Sun King" because he once danced a part with that name in a court ballet.

Louis reigned from 1643 to 1715, the longest reign of any French king. He became king when he was five years old, after the death of his father. Until 1661, France was ruled by Louis' chief minister, Cardinal Mazarin. When the cardinal died, Louis took over the throne himself.

Louis inherited a country that was weakened by foreign and civil wars. There was also rivalry among the people of his court, and his finances had been badly managed.

The young king ruled as a dictator. He believed that he had a divine right to rule. "Only God has the right to question the conduct of kings," he said. On another occasion Louis said *"L'état, c'est moi"* ("I am the state").

Within twenty years Louis had raised France to heights of prosperity and glory. His court was the most dazzling in Europe. Louis fought four wars. As a result of these France gained Flanders (modern Belgium) and some German border territory including Alsace and Lorraine.

Louis was a staunch Roman Catholic, and persecuted the Huguenots (French Protestants). About 400,000 of them emigrated, many to the Netherlands and to Brandenburg in Germany.

▲WHEN WAS THE PALACE OF VERSAILLES BUILT?

The Palace of Versailles is near Paris. It was built between 1661 and 1708, on the orders of Louis XIV. Additions were built in 1756 for Louis XV. The palace is now a museum.

The picture shows Louis XIV at Versailles, with some of his courtiers. Louis had the palace built to show off the power and wealth of his court. The palace is more than 875 yards long. It consists of a vast center section and two long wings.

There are hundreds of rooms in the palace. The most remarkable is the Hall of Mirrors, which is 240 feet long. It has windows down one side, and huge mirrors on the opposite wall.

Louis employed the finest painters, sculptors and craftsmen to decorate the palace. Formal gardens were laid out around the buildings.

In the grounds stand two smaller palaces, known as the Grand Trianon and the Petit Trianon. The Grand Trianon was built as a retreat for Louis XIV when he wanted to relax away from the court. The Petit Trianon was built by Louis XV for one of his favorites, the Comtesse du Barry.

The extravagance of Versailles caused great anger in France. People resented having to pay for the court, especially the poor peasants, who were taxed heavily. This helped to bring about the French Revolution in 1789, when Louis XVI was king.

▶ WHEN DID THE ENGLISH CIVIL WAR TAKE PLACE?

The English civil war began in 1642 and lasted until 1646.

The war was between King Charles I and his Parliament. The main cause was money. Charles did not have enough money to run the government. When Parliament tried to control his income, he ruled as a dictator. So the king's power provided a second cause for conflict.

A third cause was religion. Many people, especially in Parliament, wanted a purer form of religion. They feared that Charles favored Roman Catholicism.

The parliamentary forces were known as "roundheads" because of their short hair. They defeated the royalists, or "cavaliers," in four years and took Charles prisoner. They tried him for treason and executed him in 1649.

In 1650-51 Charles's son, Charles II, tried to recapture the throne but was defeated. In 1660, however, the monarchy was restored, with Charles II as king.

Roundhead   Cavalier

◀ WHICH TSAR MADE RUSSIA A LEADING POWER IN EUROPE?

Peter I, known as "the Great," modernized his backward country and made it a strong nation.

Peter became joint tsar with his half-brother, Ivan V, in 1682. Ivan was feeble-minded, so Peter became sole ruler in 1689, when he was 17.

In 1697-98 Peter made a tour of Western Europe. Among his companions was his tutor. Peter traveled under the name of Bombadier Peter Mikhailov – though everyone knew perfectly well who he was.

Although he met other kings and statesmen, Peter spent a lot of time studying European technology. He even worked for a week as a carpenter in a Dutch shipyard, learning how ships were built.

On his return to Russia, Peter forced his nobles to adopt Western dress and to cut off their long, shaggy beards. He built a new capital city, St. Petersburg (now Leningrad), and modernized Russia's civil service.

▶ WHEN DID MARIA THERESA RULE AUSTRIA?

Maria Theresa was ruler of Austria from 1740 to 1780, but she had to fight for her right to rule.

Maria Theresa was the only child of the Habsburg ruler of the Holy Roman Empire, Charles VI, who was also Archduke of Austria. Before he died, Charles named his daughter as his heir. He persuaded most of the other European rulers to agree that she should succeed him.

Many people did not like the idea of a woman ruler. France, Poland, Prussia, Sardinia and Saxony formed an alliance to seize her lands. Maria Theresa fought them off with help from Britain, Hungary and the Netherlands in the War of the Austrian Succession. She lost the province of Silesia to Prussia, but persuaded the German princes to choose her husband, Francis of Lorraine, as emperor. Maria Theresa tried to regain Silesia in the Seven Years' War of 1756-1763, but failed.

**The American War of
Independence broke out in
1775 and lasted until 1783.**

The war was between Britain
and its 13 North American
colonies. The colonists had
some independence, but the
British controlled their
overseas trade and their
industries.

Trouble began to develop
after the British defeated the
French in North America, and
took over their Canadian
empire. The British decided
that they must keep an army in
North America, and taxed the
colonists to pay for it.

In 1774 a congress of 12 of
the colonies agreed not to trade
with Britain until the British
changed their policies. The
following April a British force
went to seize a store of
weapons held by the colonists
at Concord, Massachusetts.
Colonial militiamen
confronted the British soldiers
at dawn. Somebody fired a
shot, and war began.

As the fighting went on,
the colonists issued the
Declaration of Independence
on July 4, 1776. They decided
to make a complete break with
Britain.

After an American victory in
1777 at Saratoga, New York
State, the French decided to
enter the war against Britain.
The Dutch and Spaniards also
joined in the following year. In
1781 a British army
surrendered at Yorktown,
Virginia, and the British then
agreed to peace talks. In 1783,
the United States of America
was recognized as an
independent country. Its first
president was George
Washington.

Danton Robespierre Marat

**The first French
Republic was declared on
September 21, 1792.
It lasted until May 18, 1804.**

The French Revolution, which
led to the declaration of a
republic, began in 1789. It
followed years of unrest caused
by great inequalities. Peasants
did not always have enough to
eat. They and the middle
classes paid heavy taxes, while
the wealthy nobles lived in
great luxury and paid little tax.

The revolution began with
the storming of the Bastille, a
prison in Paris. It continued
with the arrest of the king,
Louis XVI, and the formation
of the National Convention.
Among the convention's
leaders were Georges Danton,
Maximilien Robespierre and
Jean Marat. The convention
tried Louis for treason and had
him executed. A Committee of
Public Safety took over the
government. In a Reign of
Terror, it had thousands of its
opponents put to death.

The rebellion took place in 1791 on the island of Hispaniola in the West Indies.

In 1791 Haiti was the French colony of St. Domingue. It had a population of about 520,000, of whom 85 percent were slaves. The slaves were Africans who had been imported to work on the plantations. The white plantation owners treated the slaves badly, and also the 27,000 free *mulattos* (people of mixed Black and French ancestry).

When France was torn by revolution, the oppressed peoples seized their chance to rebel. Their leader was Pierre Dominique Toussaint L'Ouverture (shown here), one of the slaves. By 1801 Toussaint ruled the whole island of Hispaniola. Napoleon then sent an army to subdue the rebels. Toussaint was arrested and died in prison, but the people of Haiti won independence in 1804.

Napoléon made himself emperor of France in 1804. He ruled until 1814 when he was forced to abdicate.

After the chaos of the French Revolution, an ambitious soldier gained power in France. He was the successful general Napoleon Bonaparte, who came from Corsica.

Napoleon seized power on November 9, 1799, and set up a three-man government called a consulate. He was first consul and really ruled as a dictator.

Napoleon proved to be as clever a minister as he had been a general. He reorganized the government and set up a new system of laws, known as the *Code Napoléon*. In 1804 he persuaded the Senate to give him the title of emperor.

But Napoleon was ambitious, and he set out to conquer the whole of Europe. He nearly succeeded, but after years of warfare he was finally defeated at the Battle of Leipzig in 1814, and was forced to abdicate.

The "Hundred Days" lasted from March 20, 1815, to June 29. This period was Napoleon's last attempt to be the ruler of France.

After his defeat in 1814, Napoleon was exiled to the island of Elba in the Mediterranean. He was allowed to rule the island and keep his title of emperor.

In 1815 Napoleon heard that many people in France were dissatisfied with their new king, Louis XVIII. He decided to return. With 1,200 men, Napoleon landed in the south of France. The first troops sent to oppose him greeted him as their hero. He was soon back in Paris, and took power for a hundred days.

Two armies opposed Napoleon. One consisted of British, Dutch, Belgians and Germans, and one of Prussians. They met Napoleon and his army near the village of Waterloo in Belgium, on June 18. The emperor was defeated and finally exiled to St. Helena, in the South Atlantic.

55

▲ WHEN DID THE GREEKS FIGHT FOR INDEPENDENCE?

Greece fought a war of independence against Turkey from 1821 to 1829.

From 146 B.C. Greece came under Roman rule and, later, that of the Byzantine (East Roman) Empire. From the 1400s it was under the control of the Ottoman Turks.

The Greeks began longing for independence in the late 1700s. In 1770, Greeks in the Peloponnese staged a revolt with Russian help, but the Turks suppressed it harshly.

In 1814 a group called *Philiké Hetairia* (the "Friendly Band") began training fighters in the mountains, and in 1821 they started a new revolt. The Turks, with Egyptian help, tried to crush the rebellion.

In 1827 Britain, France and Russia came to the aid of the Greeks. They destroyed a Turkish fleet at the Battle of Navarino (shown here). Turkey, tied up in a war with Russia, recognized Greek independence in 1832. Greece gained extra land in the early 1900s.

▲ WHEN DID SOUTH AMERICA GAIN INDEPENDENCE?

Spain's colonies won their independence between 1809 and 1825. Brazil freed itself from Portugal in 1822. Guyana won its independence in 1966, and Surinam in 1975.

In 1808, Napoleon invaded Spain and deposed its king. This started the fight for independence by Spain's South American colonies.

The main leader of the revolution was a wealthy man named Simón Bolívar. In 1810 he began a campaign to free Venezuela, which lasted nine years. Eventually he won independence for five countries – Colombia, Ecuador, Peru, Venezuela and Upper Peru, which was renamed Bolivia after him.

Further south, the wars of independence were led by José de San Martín, who helped to liberate Argentina, Chile and Peru. Bernardo O'Higgins joined San Martín in freeing Chile. Brazil did not have to fight for its freedom.

▼WHEN WAS THE COMMUNIST MANIFESTO PUBLISHED?

The *Communist Manifesto* was published in London in February 1848. It was written by two Germans, Karl Marx and Friedrich Engels.

Marx was a young philosopher and journalist whose socialist views made it impossible for him to work in his native Germany. He sought refuge in Paris. There he met Engels, a young economist.

The two moved to Brussels, where they wrote the *Communist Manifesto*. This 24-page document was designed to present the views and policies of a new organization, the International Communist Federation.

Marx and Engels believed that the poverty and suffering experienced by many people were caused by the capitalist system of society. In this system wealth is controlled by a few people who make profits from industry and business. Marx and Engels felt that there would be more progress if the workers were in control.

▲WHEN WAS THE "YEAR OF REVOLUTIONS?"

A series of uprisings in Europe in 1848 led to it being called the "Year of Revolutions."

The revolutions came at a time of bad harvests, famine and unemployment. The growing interest in socialism and communism led many people to think that they must change their governments if things were to be improved.

The first uprising (shown here) was in France. The people of Paris wanted an increase in the number of citizens allowed to vote. When King Louis Philippe failed to act, they forced him to leave the throne, and proclaimed the Second French Republic. The Austrians were inspired by this and ousted their foreign minister, Prince Metternich.

Similar uprisings in Hungary and Sardinia won their people new constitutions, and many Italian cities drove out the Austrian troops who occupied them. There were also riots in Germany and demonstrations in Britain.

▼WHEN DID THE CITY OF ROME BECOME THE CAPITAL OF ITALY?

Although modern Italy became a unified kingdom in 1861, Rome was not part of it until 1870.

Rome has always occupied a special place in Italy. It is the home of the popes, whose headquarters are at the Vatican. Rome was also the capital of the Papal States. These lands were ruled directly by the popes.

During the revolutions of 1848, the French sent troops to Rome to protect the pope. The Italian patriot Giuseppe Garibaldi (shown here) tried to capture the city in 1862 but failed. The Italian government then tried to take over Rome but was foiled by the French.

In 1870 France was at war with Prussia and had to withdraw its troops from Rome. This enabled the Italians to take over the city unopposed. Pope Pius IX refused to agree to the loss of his possessions and regarded himself as a prisoner in the Vatican.

The United States bought extra land on three occasions, in 1808, 1853 and 1867.

The first purchase was the Louisiana Territory, a vast area of land west of the Mississippi River. It had been French, but France had given it to Spain in 1762.

The United States used the Mississippi as a highway, and was anxious to have its rivermouth port of New Orleans. In 1801, President Thomas Jefferson of the U.S. heard that Napoleon had forced the Spaniards to return Louisiana to France. He began to negotiate with the French, but without success.

In 1803, France and Britain were at war. Napoleon realized that the French might have difficulty in holding on to Louisiana during the war. He offered the Louisiana Territory to the Americans for $15 million. The United States borrowed the purchase money from English and Dutch banks.

The second purchase was the Gadsden Purchase of 1853. As a result of war with Mexico in 1848, the United States acquired a large area that was originally Spanish. But in one area the frontier was not clear. To avoid disputes over it, the U.S. bought a strip of land from Mexico. The deal was negotiated by James Gadsden, US envoy to Mexico, for $10 million.

The third purchase was Alaska, which the U.S. bought from Russia in 1867 for $7.2 million. The Russians were anxious to dispose of the land, which they used only for fur hunting.

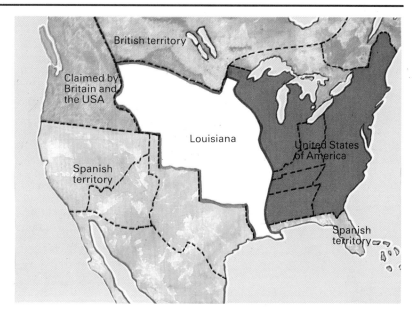

The gold rush started at the end of 1848 and reached its height during 1849.

James Wilson Marshall was a carpenter. He was hired to build a sawmill beside the American River, near Coloma in California. There, on January 24, 1848, he found nuggets of gold. The news quickly spread. Soon, Marshall's employer, John A. Sutter, found himself besieged by a horde of gold-hungry prospectors.

At first the prospectors came from California's population of 26,000. But after President James Polk announced the news, people from all over the world flocked to California. Sixty shiploads sailed from the eastern U.S. around Cape Horn. These were the first of the "49ers," as the 1849 prospectors were called. They arrived in February, but even more came overland as soon as the winter was over. By the end of 1849 California's population topped 107,000.

▼WHEN DID THE AMERICAN CIVIL WAR TAKE PLACE?

The American Civil War began on April 12, 1861, and lasted until May 26, 1865. More than 500,000 men died in the war.

The basic cause of the Civil War was slavery. The Southern states used slave labor to work in the cotton plantations. At that time there were 34 states. In 15 of these, most Black people were slaves. In the 19 states to the north, Black people were free.

In 1860, Abraham Lincoln, who opposed slavery, was elected president. At once seven Southern states withdrew and set up a new nation, the Confederate States of America. They feared that if slavery were abolished they would face economic disaster. Lincoln took action to stop this break-up of the Union, and war began.

The war led to the abolition of slavery and a victory for the North. But it left great bitterness between North and South.

▼WHEN DID THE BATTLE OF GETTYSBURG TAKE PLACE?

The Battle of Gettysburg was a turning point in the American Civil War. It lasted from July 1 to July 3, 1863.

Gettysburg is a little town in Pennsylvania, in the North. The Confederate commander, General Robert E. Lee, led an army of 75,000 men into the North. He wanted to take the fighting out of the ravaged South and perhaps force the North to start peace negotiations.

The armies maneuvered for position on July 1. Ninety thousand Union troops established their positions in the hills south of Gettysburg. On July 2 Lee's Confederate troops tried hard to capture the hills, but failed.

On July 3 Confederate troops under General George E. Pickett stormed the hills, but were too weak to hold them. Lee had to retreat, having lost 20,000 dead and wounded. He never had the strength to mount another major attack on the North.

▼WHEN DID THE BATTLE OF LITTLE BIGHORN TAKE PLACE?

The battle was fought on June 25, 1876. Sioux Indians wiped out a U.S. cavalry column led by Colonel George A. Custer.

Trouble with the Indians began in 1874 when the U.S. government broke a treaty. It sent a force of miners and soldiers into the Black Hills of South Dakota, a region sacred to the Indians. The Indians refused to sell the land, so the government decided to drive them out.

During the campaign Custer and 650 men were ordered to advance into Montana to look for an Indian village, but not to fight a major battle.

Custer found the village on the Little Bighorn River and decided to attack. He split his forces into three columns. Custer's own column fell into a Sioux ambush led by Chief Sitting Bull. Custer and his men were killed. People have argued ever since about whether Custer disobeyed orders or not.

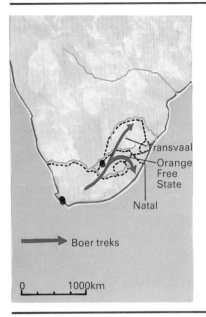

Boer treks

0   1000km

◀WHEN DID THE GREAT
TREK TAKE PLACE?

**The Great Trek was a mass
migration by Boer settlers in
South Africa in 1836 and
1837.**

The Dutch were the first
European settlers in South
Africa. They were known as
Boers, which means
"farmers." The British took
over the colony in 1814 after
the Napoleonic Wars.

The Boers did not like the
British policies. These
included making English the
official language of the colony,
and the freeing of slaves. So
the Boers decided to find a new
home where they could live as
they pleased.

In 1836 the Boers began a
massive *trek* (journey or
migration) to fresh lands
further from the sea. They
settled in the lands which are
now known as Natal, the
Orange Free State and the
Transvaal. The Transvaal was
so called because it lay across
the Vaal River. Britain later
took over Natal but recognized
the other two Boer colonies as
independent lands.

▶WHEN WAS THE ZULU
EMPIRE FOUNDED?

**The Zulus formed an empire
in Natal in the 1820s. It lasted
until 1879.**

The Zulus settled in what is
now northern Natal, probably
in the late 1600s. They began
to grow in importance under
the rule of Dingiswayo in the
early 1800s.

Dingiswayo began training a
disciplined military force.
Under his guidance the Zulu
warriors were organized into
impis (regiments), and carried
shields and *assegais* (light
spears).

Dingiswayo's successor,
Chaka, continued building the
Zulus into a military force. He
conquered Natal and
incorporated other tribes into
his empire and army. Chaka's
successor, Dingaan, came into
conflict with the Boers.

In 1873 Cetewayo became
king. He was capable, cruel
and a tyrant. He clashed with
the British and in 1879 a
British force set out to defeat
him. The Zulus won a victory
at Isandhlwana but were finally
defeated at Ulundi.

▶WHEN DID THE INDIAN
MUTINY TAKE PLACE?

**The Indian Mutiny was a
revolt by Indian soldiers in
the Bengal army against their
British officers in 1857-58.**

There were several causes for
the mutiny. Many Indians
resented changes carried out
by their British rulers, and also
the British takeover of their
territories.

The immediate cause was
the issue of new gun cartridges
that had to have the ends
bitten off before they were
fired. The cartridges were
greased, and a rumor spread
that the grease was a mixture
of pork fat or cow fat. This
shocked both the Hindu and
Muslim Indians. To Hindus
the cow is a sacred animal, and
Muslims do not touch pork.

The revolt broke out in May
1857. Indian mutineers
captured garrisons at Delhi
and Kanpur, and massacred
the British. Supported by
Sikhs, British troops put down
the mutiny fiercely.
Afterward, the British stopped
trying to change Indian ways
of life.

▼WHEN DID THE CRIMEAN WAR TAKE PLACE?

The Crimean War lasted from 1854 to 1856. It was fought by Britain, France, Sardinia and Turkey against Russia. The Crimea is a Russian peninsula on the Black Sea.

Fighting between Turkey and Russia began in 1853. One of the causes was Russia's claim to protect Christians in Palestine, which was ruled by Turkey. Russia also wanted free passage for its warships through the Turkish-held Dardanelles Strait. This links the Black Sea to the Mediterranean.

Britain and France joined the war because they thought that Russia was seizing too much of Turkey's European territory. They invaded the Crimea to attack the Russian naval base at Sevastopol.

Both sides were badly organized. More British soldiers died from disease than fighting until nursing pioneer Florence Nightingale set up proper medical care. Neither side gained much from the war.

▼WHEN DID JAPAN BECOME A MODERN POWER?

Until 1867 Japan was ruled by military governors called shoguns. Then the emperor took power and began to modernize the country.

Japan kept itself isolated from the rest of the world until a naval force arrived from the United States in 1853-54. The Americans were protesting the bad treatment of U.S. sailors who had been shipwrecked on Japanese islands. Japan signed

▲WHEN DID JAPAN DEFEAT RUSSIA?

Japan and Russia went to war in 1904 over rival claims to Manchuria and Korea. Japan's biggest victory was the naval battle of Tsushima Strait.

The Japanese began trading in Korea during the 1880s. Korea was then controlled by China. In 1894 Japan and China went to war, and Japan won control of Korea.

Japan also had eyes on the Liaotung Peninsula, in

a trade treaty with the United States and other countries.

In 1867 the Japanese emperor, Mutsuhito, gained power. He took the name *Meiji*, which means "Enlightened Rule." The Meiji government set out to modernize Japan. They abolished old customs and set up a new legal system. The Japanese built railways and a telegraph system, and started modern industries. Some Japanese people even took up Western dress and customs.

Manchuria, which Russia wanted. The Japanese offered to give up Liaotung in return for Korea, where Russia was trying to gain a foothold. When the Russians ignored their offer, the Japanese attacked. They declared war two days later.

In 1904, a peace conference was set up by the president of the United States. Japan was given the Liaotung Peninsula, half of Sakhalin Island (between Russia and Japan), and rights in Korea and Manchuria. Two years later Japan took over all of Korea.

▲WHEN WAS THE
SECOND FRENCH EMPIRE
FOUNDED?

▲WHEN WAS GERMANY
UNIFIED?

▲WHEN WAS THE PARIS
COMMUNE SET UP?

**The Second French Empire
was set up by Napoleon's
nephew Napoleon III in 1852.**

After Napoleon's downfall, the
French monarchy was
restored. When Charles X
became king he tried to make
the monarchy as powerful as it
had been before the
revolution. This caused a new
revolt in Paris in 1830. Charles
abdicated and the throne was
offered to a distant relative,
Louis Philippe.

Louis Philippe reigned for
18 years. In 1848, when his
government opposed a reform
of the voting system, the
people of Paris rebelled again
and fighting broke out. Louis
Philippe decided to abdicate.
He went in to exile in England
and a new republic was
proclaimed. Louis Napoleon,
nephew of Napoleon I, became
its first president.

Within four years the
republic also came to an end.
Louis Napoleon (shown here)
set up a Second Empire with
himself as emperor.

**The German *Reich* (Empire)
was formed in January 1871
as a result of the Franco-
Prussian War.**

Prussia was ruled by King
Wilhelm I and his Chancellor,
Otto von Bismarck. They
wanted to unite the many
states of Germany into one
country under Prussian
leadership.

Bismarck knew that a war
with France would make the
German states band together.
France and Prussia fell out
when the crown of Spain was
offered to a relative of
Wilhelm. Bismarck gave an
account of the negotiations to
the press that seemed very
insulting to the French.

France declared war on July
16, 1870. As Bismarck had
expected, the German states at
once agreed to unite. The
French were not ready for war,
and were defeated. Prussian
troops swept into France.
Wilhelm was proclaimed *kaiser*
(emperor) of Germany at
Versailles, as shown in the
picture.

**The Paris Commune was a
revolutionary council set up
after the Franco-Prussian
War in 1871.**

The Franco-Prussian War
ended with the defeat of the
main French army and the
emperor, Napoleon III. Two
days later, members of the
French Assembly proclaimed
the Third French Republic.

To make peace with
Germany, France had to pay a
huge sum of money, give up
Alsace and Lorraine, and allow
German troops to march in
triumph through Paris.

Many Parisians feared that
the new government would not
be republican enough. The
working people of the city rose
in revolt. They formed a
central committee, the
Commune, to run Paris and
lead a new revolution. But
government soldiers fought
their way into Paris. After six
weeks of fighting, and great
bloodshed, the Commune was
overthrown. The picture
shows Parisians defending the
Commune against government
troops.

▶ WHEN WAS THE MANCHU DYNASTY OVERTHROWN?

The Manchu Dynasty came to power in China in 1644. It was overthrown in 1911.

In their last years of power the Manchus had many problems. From 1842 onward, several Western nations made unfair trade treaties with China. There were also rebellions in China. The most serious of these was the Taiping Rebellion of 1851-64. In a disastrous war with Japan, in 1894-95, China also lost control of Korea and Taiwan.

The Manchus were led by the powerful empress-dowager Tz'u Hsi, who ruled on behalf of her son Kuang Hsu. They resisted change as long as they could. After 1900 the Manchus began to make sweeping reforms.

In 1908 Kuang Hsu and the empress-dowager died. A two-year-old boy, Pu-yi, became emperor. Discontent with the Manchus grew rapidly. In 1911 an uprising swept away the rule of the emperor. A republic was set up with a doctor, Sun Yat-sen, as president. Sun Yat-sen is seen here with Mrs. Sun and Chinese army officers in 1911.

▼ WHEN WERE PLANES FIRST USED IN WARFARE?

Italy used planes in the Tripolitan War of 1911. Other countries began to use warplanes in World War I.

In 1911 Italy took Libya from Turkey in the Tripolitan War. It used planes to drop bombs.

In World War I, which followed in 1914, both sides used airplanes. At first they used them for reconnaissance but soon began dropping small bombs and shooting at ground targets.

At first airplanes were used by armies and navies. Britain formed the first air force, the Royal Air Force, in 1918.

The French first used air power in 1793. They put an observer in a balloon to watch enemy troop movements during a war with Austria. The Austrians also used unmanned balloons to bomb Venice during a war in 1849.

▶ WHEN DID THE TSAR OF RUSSIA AGREE TO SWEEPING REFORMS?

Tsar Nicholas II agreed to the formation of a Duma (parliament) in 1905, following an uprising.

The uprising came as a result of Japan's defeat of Russia in the war of 1904-05. For some years there had been demonstrations calling for a democratic government, which the tsar refused to grant.

Russia's defeat in the war sparked off even bigger demonstrations. Matters came to a head on January 22, 1905, when a procession of workers and their families marched to the Winter Palace in St. Petersburg to present a petition. Police opened fire on the procession, killing 70 people and wounding 240. This incident, shown here, is called "Bloody Sunday."

Strikes, riots and mutinies of soldiers and sailors followed. The tsar had to agree to an elected parliament and other reforms. But these reforms were not enough to prevent later revolution.

◀ WHEN DID THE EASTER RISING TAKE PLACE IN IRELAND?

The rebellion began on Easter Monday, April 24, 1916 and lasted a week.

The Irish had been compaigning for independence from Britain for many years. It was finally agreed by Parliament in London, but was postponed because of World War I.

Some Irish people were not prepared to wait until the war ended. They formed a group called the Irish Volunteers. Some of the Volunteers came under the control of the Irish Republican Brotherhood, which decided on rebellion. They hoped for weapons from Britain's enemy, Germany.

The leaders of the Brotherhood decided on an Easter revolt, but the weapons they were expecting failed to appear. About 1,000 people seized the General Post Office and other buildings in Dublin. They surrendered after days of fighting. Fifteen of their leaders were shot under martial law.

▶ WHEN DID PASSIVE RESISTANCE BECOME A POLITICAL FORCE?

Passive resistance became a political force in South Africa in 1906. Later it was extended to India.

Mohandas Karamchand Gandhi was an Indian lawyer and patriot. He adopted the idea of passive resistance when he was working in South Africa and suffered racial discrimination. Gandhi later changed the name of passive resistance to *satyagraha*, which he defined as a "force which is born of truth and love or nonviolence." The aim of *satyagraha* was to bring about change without violence.

The government of the Transvaal in South Africa passed a law in 1906 requiring every Indian there to be finger-printed. In an eight-year campaign the Indians refused to obey the law, and the government repealed it.

In 1915 Gandhi returned to India. He applied his ideas of *satyagraha* there in the struggle for independence against Britain.

▶WHEN DID THE BOLSHEVIKS COME TO POWER IN RUSSIA?

The Bolsheviks seized power on the night of November 6-7, 1917.

This coup is known as the "October Revolution" because the date was October 25-26 according to the calendar then in use in Russia. This was the second revolution of 1917. The first was in March (though it is called the February Revolution). It was partly caused by the heavy defeats Russia was suffering in World War I against Germany.

The revolution began with strikes and domonstrations in which the troops joined. Tsar Nicholas II abdicated. A provisional government was formed, headed by a lawyer named Alexander Kerensky.

The Bolsheviks were a revolutionary group who thought the new government was as muddled as that of the tsar. They wanted to transform Russia along socialist lines. Their leader, Vladimir Lenin, ordered his Red Guards to seize the headquarters of the provisional government. From then on government was in the hands of *soviets* (councils) of revolutionaries. The picture shows Lenin talking at a political meeting.

▶WHEN WERE ITALY AND GERMANY RULED BY DICTATORS?

The Fascist dictator Benito Mussolini ruled Italy from 1922 to 1943. The Nazi dictator Adolf Hitler ruled Germany from 1933 to 1945.

Italy was in a state of chaos after World War I ended in 1918. There were riots, strikes, inflation, a rising crime rate, and unemployment.

Mussolini formed political clubs whose symbol was the fasces, an ax surrounded by rods. It had been the symbol of power in ancient Rome. The members became known as Fascists. Their aim was to seize power. In 1922 they converged on Rome, where Mussolini formed a government. Once in power, he became a dictator. Germany, defeated in World

War I, was in an even more disorganized state. Hitler, an agitator and orator, set up a National Socialist Party to which he rallied many discontented people of the country. Its followers were known as Nazis.

In the 1930 elections the Nazis became the second biggest party in the Reichstag, the German parliament. In 1933 the president, Paul von Hindenburg, offered Hitler the post of chancellor (premier). Within two years Hitler had murdered his rivals and made himself dictator.

65

▲ WHEN DID THE SPANISH CIVIL WAR TAKE PLACE?

The Spanish Civil War began in 1936 and lasted until 1939. It was a revolt against Spain's left-wing government.

Spain had been dogged by political unrest for many years. The election of a left-wing government in February 1936 brought matters to a head.

In July the army suddenly announced a revolution. It began in Morocco, where Spain had troops, and quickly spread to the mainland. It was headed by the army commander in the Canary Islands, General Francisco Franco. The army was supported by other right-wing groups and by the Roman Catholic Church.

Franco received help from Germany and Italy, while the government had aid from Russia. Fighting was bitter, and more than 600,000 people died. Franco's forces won.

▶ WHEN DID WORLD WAR II START?

World War II began with the German invasion of Poland on September 1, 1939.

Germany had been threatening Poland for some time. The German dictator, Adolf Hitler, wanted the so-called Free City of Danzig (Gdansk) to be united with Germany. He also wanted a link across the Polish Corridor, which allowed Poland access to the sea but cut off the main part of Germany from East Prussia.

Britain and France had pledged support for Poland. On September 3, after Poland was invaded, they declared war. They were joined by Australia, India and New Zealand. South Africa and Canada quickly followed.

In the first year of war Germany overran Poland, Denmark, Norway, Luxembourg, the Netherlands, Belgium and France. Italy joined in on Germany's side. Germany and Italy then overwhelmed Yugoslavia and Greece. Germany also attacked Russia in June 1941.

▲ WHAT HAPPENED AT PEARL HARBOR?

On the morning of December 7, 1941, Japanese bombers attacked the United States naval base (shown here) at Pearl Harbor, Hawaii. They destroyed six warships, damaged 12 others, and destroyed 174 aircraft.

The Japanese attacked while their officials were negotiating in Washington about causes of dispute between Japan and the United States. The basic cause of conflict was Japan's occupation of the French colony of Indochina (now Vietnam, Laos and Cambodia) in 1940. The U.S. government banned the sale of oil and rubber to Japan.

The Americans were caught off guard at Pearl Harbor. A telegram from Washington, warning that the Japanese might take some action, did not arrive until the attack was over. The Pearl Harbor attack took the United States into the war against Japan and its allies, Germany and Italy.

▶ WHEN DID THE BATTLE OF STALINGRAD TAKE PLACE?

The Battle of Stalingrad lasted from August 1942 to January 1943, during World War II.

The battle began as a German attempt to capture Stalingrad (now called Volgograd), a city on the Volga River. Their plan was to seize the city and sweep north to take Moscow.

The Germans slowly forced their way into the city. But the Russians resisted and fought stubbornly for every street and house. Just enough Russian reinforcements were sent into Stalingrad to keep the defense going. At the same time they assembled a huge army just north of the city.

On November 19 the Russian army attacked, and in four days surrounded the enemy. The Germans surrendered on January 31, by which time they had lost about 350,000 men.

◀ WHEN WAS D-DAY?

D-Day was the Allied landing in Normandy, France, during World War II. It took place on June 6, 1944.

The Normandy invasion was the main western attack on Germany by Britain, the U.S.A. and their allies. Three million men, 9,000 ships and 11,000 aircraft took part. After the invasion, the Germans began to retreat. The Russians also attacked from the east. Germany surrendered on May 7-8, 1945.

▶ WHEN DID THE YALTA CONFERENCE TAKE PLACE?

The Yalta Conference of 1945 was a meeting of the "Big Three" Allied war leaders. They were Winston S. Churchill of Britain, Franklin D. Roosevelt of the United States and Joseph Stalin of the Soviet Union.

The talks took place at the Crimean seaside resort of Yalta. By this time the end of the war was in sight. The Germans, fighting furiously, were being driven back by the Russians in the east and by the other allies in the west.

The purpose of the conference was to decide on the Allies' future policy toward Germany. Britain and the U.S. made a number of concessions to the Russians. They agreed to split Germany into British, Russian, French and American zones of occupation. The Russian zone is now East Germany.

▲ WHEN DID AFRICA
BECOME INDEPENDENT?

Most African countries gained their independence from Europe between the 1950s and 1970s.

European colonial powers carved up Africa among themselves during the 1800s. By 1914 only two countries were independent – Ethiopia and Liberia – though South Africa had gained almost complete freedom in 1910. Ethiopia was ruled by Italy from 1935 to 1941.

The move toward independence began as soon as World War II ended in 1945. Egypt had already become independent in 1922. Its neighbor Libya, an Italian colony, was the first to gain

freedom after the war, in 1951. Other countries to gain independence in the 1950s were Morocco, Sudan, Tunisia, Ghana and Guinea.

The main independence move came in the 1960s when 32 former colonies attained their freedom. They included almost all the French possessions in Africa.

By the early 1980s only a few African territories did not have independence. They included Namibia (South West Africa), which the United Nations had put under South African rule, and some offshore islands. The Canary Islands ranked as Spanish provinces. Madeira remained a Portuguese district. Réunion was an overseas department of France, and St. Helena remained British.

▲ WHEN DID COMMUNISTS
WIN POWER IN CUBA?

Dr. Fidel Castro, a young lawyer, led the revolution. He took power in Cuba in January 1959.

A military dictatorship led by a former army sergeant, Fulgencio Batista, held power in Cuba from 1934 to 1944 and from 1952 to 1959. Though some people prospered under his rule, most Cubans lived in great poverty.

Castro tried to start a revolution in 1953. He was captured and jailed but was released in 1955. In 1956 he returned to Cuba from exile and began a guerrilla war.

The guerrillas grew in strength until they became too much for Batista, who fled the country on January 1, 1959. Castro, shown here, set up a revolutionary government.

Cuba had strong links with the United States, which had helped to free it from Spanish rule in 1898. But relations cooled after Castro took over American businesses in Cuba. Castro then turned to the Soviet Union for military and economic help.

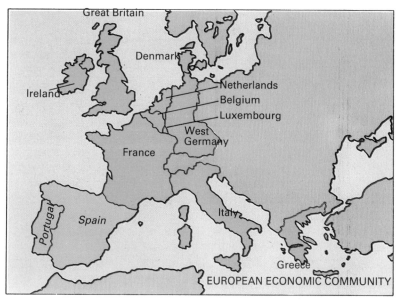

EUROPEAN ECONOMIC COMMUNITY

▲ WHEN DID EGYPT BECOME A REPUBLIC?

Egypt became a republic in 1953, following a revolt by army officers.

Egypt was part of the Ottoman Empire until 1914, when the British took control. It became an independent kingdom in 1922, but British troops stayed until 1936. After that some remained to guard the Suez Canal. This waterway was partly owned by Britain.

Egypt's king, Farouk, was an incompetent ruler who spent his life in luxury and dissipation. In 1952 a group of army officers forced him to resign in favor of his baby son, Fuad II. The commander-in-chief of the army, Muhammad Neguib, became prime minister. A year later the republic was set up with Neguib as president.

In 1954 Neguib was forced to resign. He was succeeded by Gamal Abdel Nasser (seen here), who had led the 1952 revolt. In 1956 Nasser nationalized the Suez Canal. Britain and France tried to take it back by force but were stopped by the United Nations.

▲ WHEN WAS THE EUROPEAN ECONOMIC COMMUNITY SET UP?

The European Economic Community was founded when France, Italy and four other countries signed the Treaty of Rome in 1957.

The other four countries were West Germany and the "Benelux" group – Belgium, the Netherlands and Luxembourg. The six nations had already been cooperating in the European Coal and Steel Community, set up in 1952.

The six removed trade barriers among themselves and agreed to charge the same duties on goods imported from outside the Community. They also set up a parliament and a court of justice.

In 1973 Britain, the Republic of Ireland and Denmark joined the EEC Greece was admitted in 1981.

Norway planned to join the EEC in 1973, but its people voted against it. Spain and Portugal applied to join in the early 1980s, while Greenland (part of Denmark) voted to pull out.

▶ WHEN DID THE VIETNAM WAR END?

The Vietnam War, between North and South Vietnam, ended in 1975.

Vietnam was under French rule from 1883 until World War II, when Japan took it over. After the war, the northern Vietnamese set up a communist government. From 1946 France fought the Communists. This war ended in 1954 with the partition of Vietnam into North and South Vietnam.

By 1957, North and South Vietnam were at war. Other countries sent troops. The U.S., which supported the South, had over half a million troops there by 1969. South Vietnam surrendered to the North on April 30, 1975.

SCIENCE AND TECHNOLOGY

▼HOW DID ANCIENT PEOPLES TELL THE TIME?

People first measured time in days, as night followed day. They also knew approximately how long a year lasts by observing the seasons. People could also measure time in months by watching the moon, which takes just over 27 days to return to the same position in the sky. The first instruments for measuring time were the sundial and water clock. They were invented in Egypt in about 1500 B.C.

The first sundials were simply sticks placed in the ground, with marks to indicate the time of day. It was soon found that the stick has to be placed at an angle to give the right time at different times of the year. Shadow clocks were also invented in Egypt at about the same time as the sundial. These were lengths of wood or stone marked with a scale and fixed to a raised block at one end. When the sun shone, the shadow of the top of the block fell on the scale to indicate the time.

The water clock was a vessel into which water poured at a steady rate, or a container with a hole so that water poured out of it at a steady rate. The side of the vessel or container was marked with a scale. The level of the water on the scale indicated the time.

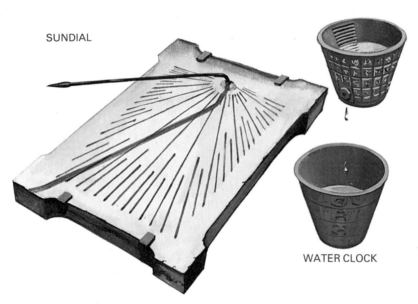

SUNDIAL

WATER CLOCK

►WHEN WAS GLASS FIRST MADE?

Glass was first made in about 3000 B.C. in Syria or nearby countries. It was probably discovered by accident when people mixed soda (a kind of salt) with hot sand on which a fire had been lit.

Before people made glass, they used a natural kind of black glass called obsidian. This glass is found near volcanoes. Stone Age people made knives, arrowheads and tools from obsidian.

The first glass containers were made by cutting into blocks of glass, or by heating the glass until it was soft and then molding it into shape. Glassblowing was discovered in about 100 B.C., probably in Syria.

In ancient times, people could not make large sheets of glass, so very few houses had glass windows. The glass vessel shown here was made in Syria during ancient Roman times.

▼WHEN DID PEOPLE BEGIN TO WEIGH THINGS?

The first device used for weighing was the balance. It was invented between 5000 and 4000 B.C. in Syria or nearby countries. People first used balances to weigh gold dust. They made stone weights that were sometimes shaped like animals.

People first began to weigh because they needed to know how much gold dust they possessed, in order to find its value. It was not until about 2500 B.C. that the balance was used to weigh other goods to measure their value for trading. Before this time, people simply bartered goods of about the same value.

The weights used in ancient balances were made of polished stone. They were in units, like ounces and pounds. They did not wear away and so were very accurate. A balance could measure the weight of an object with an error of only one per cent.

▼WHEN WAS THE WATER WHEEL INVENTED?

The water wheel was invented in about 100 B.C. in Greece. The first water wheels were placed in streams or channels of water. They turned horizontally and made a grindstone fixed above the water wheel spin to grind corn into flour.

The vertical water wheel was invented soon after the Greek water wheel. It was first described by a Roman writer in about 15 B.C. It developed from a method of raising water for irrigation. Containers were fixed to a wheel placed in a stream. The wheel was turned by people or animals to fill the containers with water and then empty them into a channel. Then paddles were fixed to the wheel so that the flow of water would make it turn. From this, people realized that water wheels with paddles, but no containers, could be used to give power. These water wheels were first used in mills to turn grindstones.

▼WHEN WAS THE PULLEY INVENTED?

A pulley is made of rope and wheels. It is used to lift heavy objects. The pulley was invented in Greece in about 450 B.C. One of its first uses was to lower an actor playing the part of a god on to a stage so that he appeared to descend from heaven.

Pulleys were also used in ancient Greece to lift and move heavy beams in shipbuilding. The famous Greek scientist Archimedes discovered how to connect pulleys together so that they could raise very heavy objects. In about 250 B.C., he demonstrated how effective they can be by using a pulley to drag a fully-laden ship ashore entirely by his own efforts. The Romans used pulleys to build cranes for lifting blocks of stone and other materials in building.

Pulleys enable people to lift heavy weights because the person using one has to pull in a long length of rope to raise an object a short distance. This has the effect of increasing the effort with which the person pulls on the rope.

BALANCE

Pan

Weights

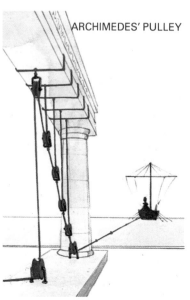

ARCHIMEDES' PULLEY

▶WHEN WERE WINDMILLS FIRST USED?

The first windmills were used in Iran in about A.D. 640. They did not look like today's windmills. The first windmills had sails similar to those on a boat. The sails were fixed to a wheel that turned horizontally, not vertically like more modern windmills. At first, the windmills were built inside towers with slots through which the wind blew on to the sails. Later the Chinese made horizontal windmills that worked in the open.

The early horizontal windmills developed from the horizontal water wheels used to power flour mills. However, they were first used to pump up water from wells to irrigate land in order to grow crops. Later the windmills were used for grinding corn to make flour.

The vertical windmill was invented in Europe, probably in England or France, in about 1170. It had several sails or huge blades to catch the wind. Provided it faced into the wind, the vertical windmill was better than the horizontal windmill because the wind blew on all the sails or blades all the time. In the horizontal windmill, the wind only pushed the sails as they moved across the wind, so it was not as powerful as the vertical windmill. Later, a second small set of blades called a fantail was added to the vertical windmill. It turned the windmill if the wind changed so that it always faced into the wind.

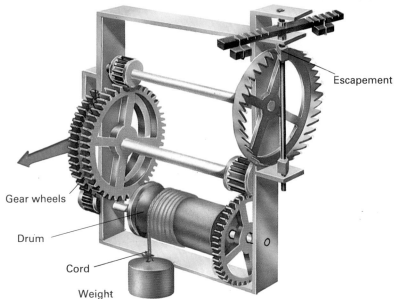

Escapement

Gear wheels

Drum

Cord

Weight

▲WHEN WERE THE FIRST MECHANICAL CLOCKS MADE?

The first mechanical clock is believed to have been made in China in A.D. 1088. It was about 33 feet high and was powered by water. In Europe, mechanical clocks were first made in the 1200s.

Early mechanical clocks made in Europe were driven by a weight on the end of a cord wound round a drum. As the drum rotated, it turned the hands of the clock. The earliest-known clock was made in Spain in 1276. The oldest mechanical clock that still works is in Salisbury Cathedral in Britain. It was made in 1368.

These clocks had devices called escapements to keep the hands turning at the correct rate, so that the clocks kept time. Even so, they were not very accurate. But this did not matter in many places because the clocks were adjusted every day at sunset, when a new day was said to begin.

◀WHEN WAS GUNPOWDER FIRST USED?

The Chinese discovered how to mix saltpeter, sulfur and charcoal together to make gunpowder. They first used it in about A.D. 850. The gunpowder was used for fireworks as well as to make rockets and explosives.

In China, gunpowder was packed into bamboo tubes to make bombs and rockets. Projectiles such as stones and pieces of broken pottery were then included. From this, the idea of using gunpowder to fire a stone ball from a cannon developed. People in Europe did not find out how to make gunpowder until the 1200s, and it began to be used in guns in the 1300s.

The invention of gunpowder was one of the most important developments of the Middle Ages. It completely changed warfare, enabling people to attack strongholds such as castles successfully.

◀WHEN WERE SPECTACLES FIRST WORN?

Spectacles were first worn in Italy in about 1285. They improved the vision of people who could not see close objects clearly. For the first time, people could continue to read if their eyesight became poor.

An Arab scientist called Alhazen found out how lenses produce images in about 1000. He showed that a magnifying glass can be used to see close objects clearly. From this, the idea of spectacles developed. At first, people wore them with the two lenses placed very close together. This was because they thought that light rays come to the center of the face before reaching the eyes. It was some time before people realized that the lenses should go over the eyes.

Spectacles that allow people with short sight to see distant objects clearly were invented in Italy in about 1430.

▶WHEN WAS THE MAGNETIC COMPASS INVENTED?

The magnetic compass points north. It was invented in China in about A.D. 1000, and came into use in Europe about 100 years later. The first compass was a magnetized iron needle placed on a piece of cork or straw floating in a dish of water.

In about 100 B.C. the Chinese discovered that if spoons made of the magnetic mineral lodestone were spun, they came to rest with the handles pointing in the same direction. This was because the earth's magnetic field acted on the spoons like a compass. The compass developed from this observation.

The form of compass we have today consists of a pivoted magnetic needle on a card with directions. It was invented in the 1200s. Using the magnetic compass, explorers were able to find their way more easily and to draw much better maps.

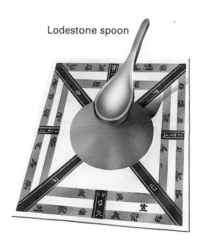

Lodestone spoon

▶ WHEN WERE THE FIRST BOOKS PRINTED?

The first books were printed in China and Korea in about A.D. 700. The earliest ones known are scrolls in which the writing was printed with wooden blocks. It took a long time for printing to reach Europe. There books were first printed in Germany in about 1450.

Paper and ink were also invented in China. Printing books became possible with the invention of movable type – separate blocks of wood each with a letter or symbol that could be put together to print writing. Type made of porcelain was invented in China in about 1050, and then metal type was invented in Korea.

In Europe, Johann Gutenberg of Mainz, in

AN EARLY EUROPEAN PRINTING PRESS

Germany, began to use metal type and a printing press to print books in about 1450. The first full-length printed book was the Gutenberg Bible of about 1454. Only 21 copies of this book now exist.

Books were written out by hand before printing began, so were rare and expensive. With the invention of printing, books became cheaper and plentiful. People were able to read much more and knowledge spread rapidly.

PASCAL'S CALCULATOR

▲ WHEN WAS THE FIRST CALCULATOR MADE?

The first instrument to help people make calculations was the abacus. This has beads that are moved along wires in a frame to represent numbers. It developed in Babylonia in about 3000 B.C. The first calculating machine was invented in France in 1642. It could add and subtract numbers automatically.

The first calculating machine was built by the French scientist Blaise Pascal at the age of 19. Numbers were fed into the calculator by operating wheels. These wheels turned gears inside the calculator. The gears then moved dials with numbers so that the result showed in a set of windows. The calculator worked well but it could only add and subtract numbers. The first calculating machine that could also multiply and divide was invented by the German scientist Gottfried Leibnitz, in 1694.

Mechanical calculating machines based on the same principles as these first calculators were used until the 1970s. Electronic calculators then became widespread.

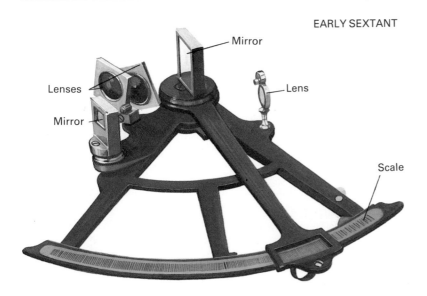

EARLY SEXTANT

Mirror

Lenses

Lens

Mirror

Scale

the North Star is above the horizon. The navigator looks through lenses and mirrors fixed to the sextant, and views the sun or star and the horizon. A scale on the sextant then gives the height of the sun or star. From this and the time of the observation, the navigator can work out the position.

Accurate clocks were also developed during the 1700s. By using them with the sextant, navigators on ships at sea were able to find their correct position for the first time.

The sextant was first thought of by Sir Isaac Newton. He suggested that a simple observing instrument called a quadrant could be improved by fixing a telescope to it.

▲ WHEN WAS THE SEXTANT FIRST USED?

The sextant is an instrument that navigators use to find their position. With a sextant, they can observe the sun or a star in the sky to work out where they are on the earth.

The sextant was invented by John Hadley of Britain and Thomas Godfrey of the United States in 1731. It made navigation easier, and sea travel became safer.

The sextant measures how high the sun or a star such as

▶ WHEN WAS COAL GAS FIRST USED?

Coal gas was first made in Britain in 1727. In 1760, George Dixon used the gas for the first time to light a room in his house at Durham. The gas light was much brighter than the light of oil lamps or candles. However, after a gas explosion, Dixon stopped his experiments.

Coal gas is made by heating coal in closed ovens. The process was rather dangerous. William Murdock and other British scientists found safe ways of using gas for lighting homes. Gas lighting made a big difference to people's lives. In 1807, gas began to be used for street lighting in London, making the city a safer place. From 1805, it was also used to light factories so that they

could continue producing goods at night. Gas lighting also allowed people to gain education after work at evening classes.

From 1802 onward, beginning in Germany, coal gas was also used for heating

homes and as a fuel for stoves. It later became a valuable source of chemicals for industry.

▶WHEN WERE STEAM ENGINES FIRST USED?

The first successful steam engine was made by the British engineer Thomas Newcomen in 1712. It was used to pump water out of mines. James Watt later improved Newcomen's engine. He is said to have been inspired by watching steam lift a kettle lid.

The steam engine had a large cylinder connected to a beam. Steam was fed into it to make a piston rise and fall. Beginning in 1765, James Watt made the steam engine work faster and with more power. He also made it drive machines. Watt steam engines were first put to work in cotton mills in 1785. Powered by steam engines, industries then developed in cities. Steam engines were also used for transportation, beginning with the first steamboat in France in 1783 and the invention of the locomotive in Britain in 1803.

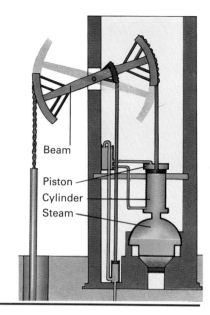

Beam
Piston
Cylinder
Steam

NEWCOMEN'S STEAM ENGINE

▶WHEN WERE THE FIRST SPINNING MACHINES INVENTED?

Spinning machines were invented in Britain in the 1700s. Before then, people used to spin thread by hand. They pulled fibers out of cotton and wool and twisted them into thread. The spinning machines had rollers turning at different speeds to twist the fibers into yarn.

The first successful spinning machine was the hand-powered spinning jenny built by James Hargreaves in 1764. It produced thin yarn. Richard Arkwright's water frame of 1769 (so called because it was powered by water wheels) gave a sturdy thread. In 1779, Samuel Crompton combined these two spinning machines to make the spinning mule, which could spin several kinds of yarn. By increasing the production of thread, these machines created the textile industry and began the Industrial Revolution.

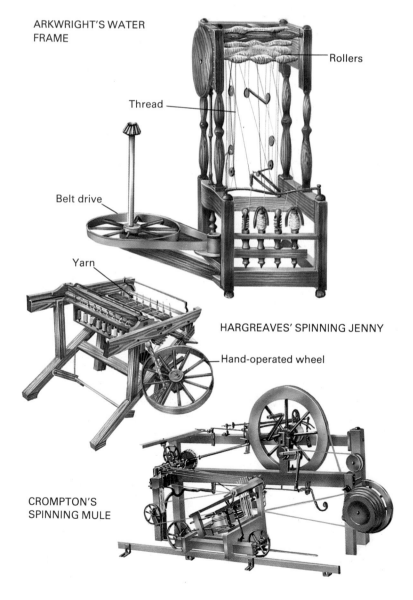

ARKWRIGHT'S WATER FRAME

Rollers

Thread

Belt drive

Yarn

HARGREAVES' SPINNING JENNY

Hand-operated wheel

CROMPTON'S SPINNING MULE

COTTON GIN

Comb

Teeth

Cylinder

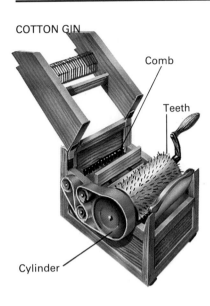

JACQUARD LOOM

Punched cards

Woven cloth

1 Molten iron

2 Burning carbon

BESSEMER CONVERTER

3

Molten steel

▲ WHEN WAS THE COTTON GIN INVENTED?

Eli Whitney invented the cotton gin in the United States in 1793. Before then, cotton was plucked from cotton plants by hand. The cotton gin did this work more efficiently, so more cotton could be produced to make cloth.

Cotton plants have bolls, which are masses of seeds and cotton fibers. In the cotton gin, the bolls were fed to a toothed cylinder which was turned to pull the fibers away from the seeds.

The cotton gin could be worked by hand, horse or water power. It provided the great amount of cotton needed by the growing textile industry. The industry had been revolutionized by the invention of spinning machines and powered looms, which made thread and wove cloth in large quantities.

In 1798 Eli Whitney introduced mass production into factories. His machines, made muskets in great quantities at high speed.

▲ WHEN WERE AUTOMATIC MACHINES INVENTED?

The first automatic machine was a loom that could weave patterns in silk cloth. It was invented in France in 1801. Before this time, people had to control the machines that they used. The automatic loom could weave any pattern unaided.

The automatic loom was invented by Joseph Marie Jacquard. Cards punched with holes were fed into the loom to make it weave a particular pattern. Needles moved through the holes and caused hooks to lift some of the threads in the loom and weave the pattern required. A new pattern could be woven by feeding a different set of punched cards into the loom.

This idea of punched card control of machines had been thought of before in France, but Jacquard was the first to use it successfully. It was later very important in the development of computers.

▲ WHEN WAS STEEL FIRST MADE?

Steel was first made in Britain in about 1740. It was produced at Sheffield by Benjamin Huntsman. Steel is made from iron, but is stronger than iron. Huntsman's steel was expensive because his process could not make large amounts. A way of manufacturing steel cheaply was invented over a century later.

The British engineer Henry Bessemer invented a method of producing steel in large quantities in 1856. He put molten iron in a large vessel called a converter and then blew air through it. This made most of the carbon impurities in the iron burn, turning the iron into steel. The converter was then tipped and the molten steel flowed out.

In the United States, William Kelly developed the same steel-making process before Bessemer. But he kept it secret for too long and Bessemer announced his invention first.

ELIAS HOWE'S SEWING MACHINE

◀WHEN WERE SEWING MACHINES FIRST USED?

The sewing machine was invented by Barthelemy Thimmonier in France, in 1830. It could sew 200 stitches in a minute. However, tailors who thought that the sewing machine would put them out of work started a fire which destroyed it.

The first successful sewing machine was made by Elias Howe in the United States in 1845. Unlike today's machines, the cloth was held upright and the needle moved horizontally. In 1851, also in the United States, Isaac Singer developed the kind of sewing machine we use today.

The invention of the sewing machine made a great impact on people's lives. It created a huge clothing industry that produced good cheap clothes for all. With sewing machines, articles such as boots and shoes, saddles and harnesses, umbrellas and mattresses could also be manufactured. Bookbinding also became an industry.

▶WHEN WERE HARVESTING MACHINES INVENTED?

There are two kinds of harvesting machines. Reapers cut down the corn, and threshers get the grains of corn out of the ears of corn. Both jobs were once done by hand. People used to cut corn with sickles or scythes and thresh it in their fingers.

The first threshing machine was invented in Britain by Andrew Meikle in 1786. A spinning drum inside the thresher rubbed the grains from the ears of corn. The first reaping machine was invented by Patrick Bell in Britain in 1826. It had large blades that turned to push the corn into a row of cutters like scissors.

In Meikle's threshing machine, the corn was fed into a container with a rotating drum. It was pulled into a narrow space between the drum and walls of the container, which stripped away the grains of corn. To help separate the grain from the chaff (the bits of stalks and

McCORMICK'S REAPER

ears of corn), Meikle added sieves to capture the chaff, and fans to blow it away.

Bell's reaping machine was *pushed* by horses into a field of corn so that they did not trample down the corn first. This did not work well. The first successful reaping machine was made by Cyrus McCormick in the United States in 1831. McCormick's reaper was *pulled* by horses walking alongside the corn to be cut. Rotating blades pushed the corn into a cutter bar with a sliding knife that sliced the stalks.

Harvesting machines developed mainly in the United States because there were huge areas of land to be harvested. Threshers were powered at first by steam. Reapers were drawn by tractors. Combine harvesters that reap and thresh the corn in one operation were invented later. They separate the grain and place it in containers, while the stalks are bound into bales of straw.

▶WHEN WAS THE ELECTRIC MOTOR INVENTED?

The first person to make an electric motor was Michael Faraday, in 1821. He is shown here with the motor. His motor was only experimental and could not be used. The first practical electric motor was invented in 1873.

It took a long time to invent an electric motor to drive machines because a powerful source of electricity was required. This did not become available until the Belgian engineer Zenobe-Theophile Gramme invented the dynamo in 1870. He then built the first practical electric motor three years later.

Motors of this kind, which use direct current, powered the first electric streetcars and trains in Germany in 1881. Alternating current motors were invented in the United States by Nikola Tesla in 1888. They use the electricity supply, which began operation in the United States in 1882.

◀WHEN WAS THE FIRST ELEVATOR USED?

The first elevator for taking people from one floor to another was used in 1743. It was built for King Louis XV of France. The safety elevator, which stops if the rope holding it should break, was invented in 1853 by the American engineer Elisha Otis.

Hoists and cranes to raise loads were invented in ancient times. They were not needed for people until about a century ago because buildings were not very tall. Louis XV's elevator was installed at the Palace of Versailles for his private use so that he could not be seen. It was balanced by weights and was raised or lowered by hand.

The safety elevator had teeth along the shaft. If the rope broke, a bar sprang out of the side of the elevator. It engaged in the teeth and stopped the elevator from falling down the shaft. In the picture Otis demonstrates his safety elevator at the New York exhibition of 1853.

▶WHEN WERE THE FIRST SKYSCRAPERS BUILT?

Skyscrapers are high buildings with many floors. The first one (seen here) had ten floors. It was built in Chicago in 1883. After the safety elevator was invented in 1853, tall buildings could be built because people did not have to climb the stairs.

The first skyscraper was the Home Insurance Building in Chicago. It was built by William Le Baron Jenney. The building (now demolished) had a frame of iron and steel beams, which made the structure light but strong. Buildings made of brick could not exceed 14 floors because the walls would have had to be enormously thick to support the weight of the building. The highest structure of this time was the Eiffel Tower in Paris, which was built of steel beams in 1889 to a height of 990 feet. It is still one of the highest structures in the world.

▲ WHEN WAS THE FIRST ARTIFICIAL DYE MADE?

The first artificial dye was made in 1856. The British scientist William Perkin discovered how to make a mauve dye. Before this discovery, all dyes were made from plants and insects. No more than about 12 colors were commonly used. Artificial dyes in many different colors were made after Perkin's discovery.

William Perkin discovered mauve by accident at the age of only 18. Working at home, he was trying to prepare the drug quinine from a chemical called aniline. Perkin made a black sludge that dissolved in water to produce a beautiful purple color. The solution would dye silk, and Perkin found a way of using it so that it could also dye cotton. Unlike natural purple dyes such as lilac colors, Perkin's mauve (as it was called) did not wash out and did not fade. It began a fashion for mauve garments and Perkin became a successful dye manufacturer.

Dyes have complex molecules and before Perkin's accidental discovery, chemists did not know how to make them. Many more artificial dyes were then produced.

▼ WHEN WAS PHOTOGRAPHY INVENTED?

The first photograph (shown here) was taken in France in 1826. It is a view of a courtyard taken by Joseph Niepce. It took eight hours to make the exposure! This photograph was not made in the same way as today's photographs. The British scientist William Fox Talbot invented modern photography in about 1835. His pictures were black and white.

Niepce's photograph was made with a layer of bitumen on a metal plate. After the eight-hour exposure, the bitumen was washed in oil. The light had hardened the bitumen in the light parts of the picture. Only the dark parts of the picture washed away so the dark metal showed through to give a picture.

In 1837, Louis Daguerre of France invented a method of taking photographs called daguerrotypes. These were the first clear and permanent photographs, but only one picture could be made of a scene. It was not possible to produce copies. Fox Talbot invented the process of making a negative from which positive prints can be made. Later inventions were the first color photograph in 1861 and the first photographic film in 1881, both made in Britain.

▼WHEN WERE THE FIRST OIL WELLS DRILLED?

Oil was first discovered by drilling in 1841, in the United States. It was found by accident when drilling for salt. The first well that was drilled on purpose to find oil was constructed in the United States in 1859.

Before oil wells were drilled, people obtained oil at places where the oil flowed naturally to the surface. In 1854, oil seeping out of the ground at Titusville, Pennsylvania, was tested by scientists at Yale University. They found it to be full of useful substances such as gasoline, kerosene and lubricating oils.

Edwin Drake built the first well to bring this oil up from underground. He inserted a hollow shaft into the ground so that the oil could flow up the shaft. On August 28, 1859, Drake struck oil at a depth of 70 feet and oil gushed from the well. This was the beginning of today's great oil industry.

▼WHEN WAS GASOLINE FIRST PRODUCED?

Gasoline was first produced in about 1864. It was obtained from the oil that was discovered a few years before. However, gasoline was not of much use until the automobile was invented in 1883. The first gasoline station opened in France in 1895.

Gasoline is made from oil in a refinery. The oil is heated to produce gasoline vapor, and the gasoline vapor condenses to give gasoline. The refinery also produces other useful oil products such as kerosene and lubricating oils.

The first refineries were built in the United States in the 1860s, following the discovery of oil in Pennsylvania. John D. Rockefeller entered the oil business in 1862 and founded a refinery at Cleveland. In 1870, he organized the Standard Oil Company, which grew to become the largest oil company in the world. Methods of treating oil to produce gasoline developed from 1890.

▼WHEN WAS THE ELECTRIC LIGHT INVENTED?

The first kind of electric light was the electric arc. It was a continuous electric spark. Humphry Davy produced the first electric arc in Britain in 1802. However, it was too bright to be used in houses. Electric light bulbs began to be used in 1880.

Electric light bulbs contain a wire filament that glows when an electric current passes through it. This kind of electric light was invented in the U.S. in 1845 by J. W. Starr. In 1860, the British scientist Joseph Swan tried to improve this bulb without much success.

The American inventor Thomas Edison produced a successful light bulb in 1879. He used a filament of carbon made from cotton thread. Swan produced a similar bulb the next year and both men then began to manufacture light bulbs. Wire filament bulbs came into use in 1898.

DRAKE'S OIL WELL

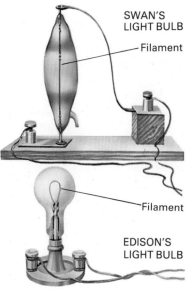

SWAN'S LIGHT BULB

Filament

Filament

EDISON'S LIGHT BULB

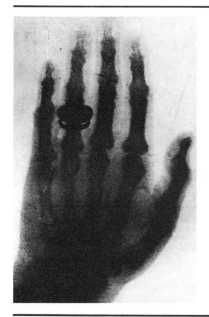

◄WHEN WERE X RAYS DISCOVERED?

X rays were discovered in 1895 by the German scientist Wilhelm Roentgen. He found them by accident. Roentgen was experimenting with a cathode-ray tube, an early form of the tube used today in television sets. One day he noticed that some crystals in the room glowed with light when the tube was switched on. This was because the tube produced X rays.

Roentgen covered the cathode-ray tube with cardboard and found that the crystals still glowed. He took the crystals into the next room and still the crystals glowed. Roentgen realized that the tube was producing invisible rays that could penetrate even walls.

Roentgen knew of no other rays like this. He called them X rays because in science X is often used to stand for something that is unknown. Roentgen soon discovered that X ray photographs show the bones inside the body.

►WHEN WERE PLASTICS INVENTED?

The first plastic was a material called Parkesine. It was invented by a British scientist called Alexander Parkes. He discovered the plastic in about 1860 when seeking a substitute for horn obtained from animals. It was used to make objects such as door knobs.

Parkesine was made from cellulose and camphor, which are natural materials obtained from plants. An American inventor called John Hyatt discovered the same plastic in 1868 when seeking a substitute for ivory. He called it celluloid, the name it has today. Another early plastic made from cellulose was artificial silk, invented by the British scientist Joseph Swan in 1883.

The first plastic to be made from chemicals was Bakelite, which was invented by the Belgian chemist Leo Baekeland in 1907. This was the first material that was totally artificial.

◄WHEN WERE TELEPHONES FIRST USED?

The telephone was invented in the United States by Alexander Graham Bell (shown here) in 1876. The first telephones were used in Boston in 1877, and the first public call box was installed in Connecticut in 1880. The first automatic telephone exchange opened at La Porte, Indiana, in 1892.

Other people in the United States also invented telephones, notably Antonio Meucci in 1854 and Elisha Grey in 1876. However, Bell was judged to be the inventor of the telephone in court actions contesting his claim to have invented it.

Bell invented the telephone when trying to find a way of helping deaf people to hear. His telephone gave the clearest speech. However, no one was interested in it until the emperor of Brazil tried the telephone and exclaimed, "My God – it talks!" The telephone then became an immediate success.

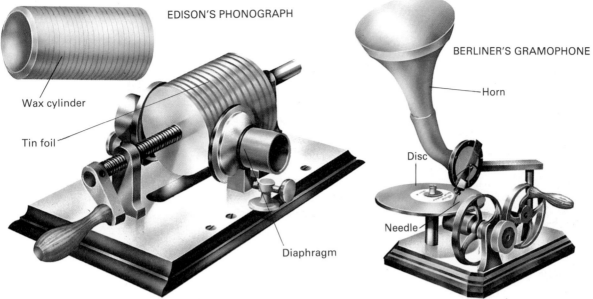

EDISON'S PHONOGRAPH

Wax cylinder

Tin foil

Diaphragm

BERLINER'S GRAMOPHONE

Horn

Disc

Needle

▲WHEN WAS THE RECORD PLAYER INVENTED?

The record player was invented by the American inventor Thomas Edison in 1877. It was called a phonograph and played cylinders instead of disks. The first recording was of Edison himself reciting *Mary Had a Little Lamb*. The gramophone, which plays flat disks and not cylinders, was invented by a German, Emile Berliner, in 1887.

Edison used a cylinder with a layer of soft tinfoil. He spoke into the machine, causing a diaphragm (plate) connected to a needle to vibrate. The cylinder rotated so that the vibrating needle cut a groove in the tinfoil. To play back the recording of his voice, the cylinder was turned and the needle placed in the groove. The needle then vibrated the diaphragm, which gave out the sound.

Edison's phonograph could not reproduce music or speech very well. An improved

instrument using wax cylinders was produced by Edison and others in 1888, and a large horn was used to amplify the weak sound given by the diaphragm.

The gramophone, which plays disks instead of cylinders, first appeared in 1889 in Germany. It was not until 1898 that copies of disks were made in quantities. Before then, the performers had to record a song or piece of music over and over again to make enough records to sell to the public.

▶WHEN DID RADIO BROADCASTING BEGIN?

The first radio broadcast to contain speech and music was made on December 24, 1906, in the United States. The broadcast was given by the Canadian inventor Reginald Fessenden. The first radio station began operating in New York in 1907.

Radio waves were discovered by the German scientist Heinrich Hertz in 1887. The Italian inventor Guglielmo

Marconi began experimenting with radio in 1894. He first sent messages consisting of morse signals in 1895. In 1901 he succeeded in transmitting signals across the Atlantic Ocean (see photograph).

Reginald Fessenden began experiments in sound radio broadcasting in 1900. In the first broadcast of 1906, Fessenden talked, sang, recited and played the violin. The first radio station opened the following year. At first it only broadcast records of popular music.

▼WHEN WAS TELEVISION INVENTED?

The first television picture was produced by the British inventor John Logie Baird in 1924. It was a still picture of a cross that he transmitted a distance of 10 feet. Baird's system is not the electronic television system that we use today. Electronic television was invented in the United States in 1927 by Philo Farnsworth.

Baird invented a mechanical system of television in which the picture was formed by a spinning disk. In 1925, Baird produced the first color pictures, first television recording and the first international transmission.

However, the mechanical system gave a small, fuzzy picture. Electronic television was developed in the United States by the engineer Vladimir Zworykin (shown here) during the 1930s. It soon replaced the mechanical system. The first public television service of the kind we have today began in Britain in 1936.

▼WHEN WAS NUCLEAR POWER FIRST PRODUCED?

Nuclear power was first produced by the Italian scientist Enrico Fermi in the United States in 1942. Fermi built the first nuclear reactor at Chicago. In the reactor, uranium was used to produce heat. This kind of reactor is used in nuclear power stations today.

To produce nuclear power, atoms of uranium or some other element must break apart. This process is called nuclear fission and it produces immense energy. Nuclear fission was discovered in 1939, just before World War II.

Scientists worked hard in the U.S. during the war to make a reactor in which nuclear fission could be controlled. Fermi succeeded in 1942. Uncontrolled nuclear power is also produced in the atomic bomb. The first such bomb was tested in the United States in 1945. Two bombs were then dropped on the cities of Hiroshima and Nagasaki in Japan.

▼WHEN WAS RADAR INVENTED?

Radar was invented during the 1930s. Scientists in several countries worked on radar at this time. The first successful radar system was produced in Britain in about 1935.

During World War II, radar stations around the coast of Britain helped to warn of the arrival of enemy aircraft. Without radar, it is possible that Germany might have defeated Britain.

Radar works by sending out radio signals that bounce off distant objects. The radar set detects the signals that return and produces a picture indicating the position of the objects.

British and American scientists worked together to invent methods of using very short radio waves called microwaves. With microwaves, small but very accurate radar sets could be installed in ships and aircraft, as well as on land. They gave Britain and America superiority over German and Japanese forces.

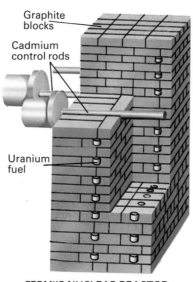

Graphite blocks

Cadmium control rods

Uranium fuel

FERMI'S NUCLEAR REACTOR

►WHEN WAS THE FIRST COMPUTER MADE?

The first computer was a machine called *Colossus* **(seen here). It was invented in Britain in 1943 during World War II. This computer was built in total secrecy. It solved messages sent out in codes by the German forces. The codes were so difficult to break that only the computer could solve them.**

Colossus was an electronic computer very like today's computers. But instead of microchips, it contained 2,000 electronic tubes. These enabled it to work very quickly in making the complex calculations needed to break the German codes.

However, unlike modern computers, *Colossus* could not be programmed to carry out any other task but code-cracking. The first general-purpose computer, which could perform different tasks, was the American computer ENIAC. It contained 19,000 tubes and first came into operation in 1946.

INDUSTRIAL ROBOT

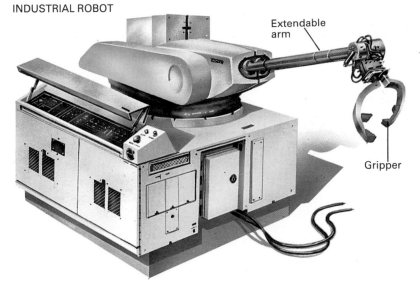

Extendable arm

Gripper

▲WHEN WERE ROBOTS INVENTED?

The first kind of robots to look and work like a mechanical person were invented during the 1700s in Europe. They were used as toys. One of the best was a writing robot built by the Swiss clockmaker Pierre Jacquet-Droz in 1770. It could write any message of up to 40 letters in handwriting.

The word "robot" was invented by the Czech playwright Karel Capek for his play *Rossum's Universal Robots*. It means "forced labor" in Czech. The play was about machines that looked and worked like human beings. In fact, the kind of robots he envisaged have never been made.

Industrial robots are machines with mechanical arms ending in hand-like gripping devices. They were developed during the 1960s for performing routine tasks in factories. Moving computer-controlled figures that look and talk like people have also been made for entertainment.

▼WHEN WAS THE LASER INVENTED?

The laser was invented in 1960 by the American scientist Theodore Maiman (seen here). The first laser produced a beam of red light.

The American scientist Charles Townes first thought of the principle of the laser in 1951. In 1953 he invented the maser – a kind of laser that produces invisible microwaves instead of light. Maiman developed Townes's ideas to invent the laser.

HOW PEOPLE LIVE

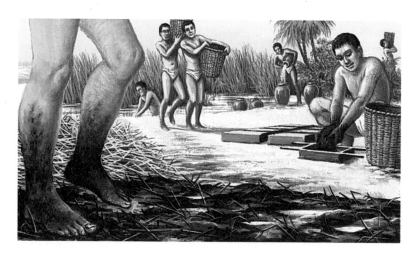

Bricks were first made over 6,000 years ago. They were shaped from wet mud and dried in the sun's heat.

Brick-making began on the river banks of the Near East and Mesopotamia. The bricks we use today are probably not very different in size from those used in ancient times. Each brick was made just big enough for someone to pick up and lay easily.

The wet mud from the river was mixed with straw for greater strength. A wooden mold was used to make each brick the same size. In the city of Ur (in what is now Iraq) an arch of bricks, held together by mortar, was built around 4000 B.C. The builders of Babylon decorated their bricks, making wall-pictures or mosaics.

Later, bricks were hardened by baking them in a kiln, or oven, in the same way as pottery is baked. Brick houses were stronger, and so could be made larger than houses made from clay or wood.

Drains were not needed until people started to live in towns. Before then, fresh water came from springs and rivers. But crowded towns needed drains to bring in fresh water, and sewers to carry away waste.

The people of ancient India, China and Rome built good water supply systems. They even had public baths. The picture shows the Great Bath at Mohenjo Daro, in Pakistan. This city was built about 4,000 years ago.

In Europe, in the Middle Ages, most towns were dirty and smelly. Waste ran through the streets in open gutters. Few houses had running water or proper lavatories, and people spilled their rubbish into the nearest river.

By the 1800s the River Thames in London smelled so bad that it made people feel ill. Even worse, there were outbreaks of deadly diseases. At last, proper water supplies and drainage systems were built to keep the cities clean and healthy.

▼WHEN WERE OIL LAMPS FIRST MADE?

Fat burns, and seeing this probably caused a cave dweller to try making the first oil lamp. Animal fat and oil gave people light for thousands of years, until an improved kind of oil lamp was invented.

Simple oil lamps must have cheered people in the darkness of a Stone Age cave. The Eskimos of the Arctic used saucer-shaped oil lamps until quite recently. The oil (from a seal's blubber) soaks into a wick of moss, and the wick burns until all the oil is used up.

The Romans burned petroleum in their lamps. In the 1680s oil lamps were hung to light London's streets.

In 1784 a Swiss named Aimé Argand invented an improved oil lamp. It had a glass chimney to shield the wick, and it gave a much brighter light. In the 1800s many homes were lit only by kerosene lamps. Gas and electric lighting were introduced later.

▼WHEN WERE CARPETS FIRST MADE?

The first floor coverings were mats woven from rushes. Weaving skills were later used to make rugs and carpets from wool. The finest carpets were richly patterned and very valuable.

Carpets made more than 2,000 years ago have been found in tombs in Asia. Most carpets are made from sheep's wool, but in Persia the finest carpets were woven in silks.

Beautifully patterned carpets made in Persia, China and Turkey were traded with other countries. The best carpets were too good to walk on, so rich people hung them on the wall. Princes often exchanged fine carpets as gifts.

All carpets were woven by hand until the 1700s, when factory machines were invented to do the work more quickly. European carpet-makers often copied Asian patterns. Since the 1700s European carpets such as Savonnerie (France) and Axminster (Britain) have become world-famous.

▼WHEN WERE KNIVES AND FORKS FIRST USED?

Cheap factory-made knives and forks appeared on dining tables in the 1800s. Before then, only rich people used them. Most people ate with their fingers.

People carried knives to kill and skin animals. At meals, they cut up meat and put it into their mouths on the point of a knife. In the Middle Ages travelers took their own knives with them. Only at a rich person's table would a guest expect to be offered a knife.

Table forks were even less common until the 1700s. The first forks had only one prong and were used for serving food. The Romans (shown here) sometimes used two-pronged forks. By the 1700s a traveler could buy a knife, fork, spoon and mug in a special case. By the 1800s most homes had factory-made table cutlery.

Of course, not everyone uses forks. Chinese chopsticks do the same job just as well – in skilled hands.

►WHEN WAS FOOD FIRST CANNED TO PRESERVE IT?

Canned foods are part of modern living, yet before the 1800s they were unknown. Most foods had to be eaten fresh, before they started to go bad. In the 1820s the first canned foods went on sale.

Since ancient times people have dried meat and fish to preserve them. Salting or pickling were also used to stop food going bad. Sailors on ocean voyages lived on a boring and unhealthy diet of salt meat and stale biscuits. The absence of fresh fruit and vegetables caused a disease called scurvy, which was common among sailors.

In the 1800s the French emperor Napoleon called on scientists to find a better means to feed a large army on the march. Napoleon wanted his soldiers to be well fed while fighting far from home. In 1809 Nicolas Appert of Paris discovered that food would keep longer if it was boiled and stored inside a sealed glass jar. Soldiers then carried bottles of preserved food with them, and no longer had to find food as they marched.

In the 1820s foods preserved in metal cans appeared in the stores for the first time. By the 1840s canned foods were popular, yet it was not until the 1860s that the first efficient can opener was invented. Until then, cans had to be opened with a hammer and chisel!

Even after canned foods had been invented, no one knew why food went bad. Louis Pasteur, a French scientist, finally showed that decay was caused by bacteria. Boiling food in jars or cans killed the bacteria, and so kept food fresh.

▲WHEN DID COFFEE-DRINKING BECOME POPULAR?

In the 1650s the new craze of coffee drinking hit Europe. Coffee houses opened in cities and fashionable people hurried to try the new drink.

The Africans and Arabs were the first to make and drink coffee. Coffee beans grew in Ethiopia and southern Arabia. After coffee drinking became popular in Europe, coffee plantations were started in South America and Asia.

People in Europe liked to meet and talk in taverns. In the mid-1600s city-dwellers took to meeting in the new coffee houses. They discussed business, art and politics. Famous writers led the conversation in the smartest coffee houses.

The coffee houses became like clubs or offices. Lloyds of London, the famous insurance business, started as a coffee house in the 1680s. The people who met there were interested in shipping, and in time Lloyds became the center for shipping news.

▲ WHEN WAS THE FIRST SUPERMARKET OPENED?

The first supermarkets, selling all kinds of goods in a single store, opened in the U.S. in the 1930s. In some places supermarkets have driven smaller stores out of business.

Small stores, such as butchers, fish dealers and vegetable shops, have been around for hundreds of years. They began as market stalls in streets.

The first department store, offering many goods beneath one roof, was opened in Paris in 1860. Supermarket chains date from 1930, when an American called Michael Cullin opened the first self-service food supermarket.

Supermarkets spread to many other countries. Often large supermarkets are built on the edge of cities, where people can park their cars easily. Inside, the shoppers collect the goods from open shelves, instead of being served by an assistant. Supermarkets therefore save money on staff and can offer cheaper prices.

◄ WHEN WERE CASH REGISTERS FIRST USED?

If a store is very busy, it is useful to have machines to keep count of each sale. Cash registers to do this first appeared on store counters in the late 1800s.

The first cash register was made in 1879 by an American saloon owner called James Ritty. His machine could add dollars and cents. Ritty got the idea by looking at a counter in a ship's engine-room. It counted the number of times the propeller shaft revolved.

Many store clerks were suspicious of the new cash registers, but store owners liked them. By the 1890s there were registers which gave the customer a paper receipt and kept count of all the sales on a paper roll. Today the latest cash registers are connected to computers, to record every item a store sells.

▲ WHEN DID FROZEN FOOD FIRST APPEAR?

Frozen foods, ready to eat, first appeared in the 1920s. But people had known about refrigeration long before.

Before people had freezers, they stored winter ice in stone ice-houses. The Romans made ice cream. A method of making artificial ice was invented in 1834 by Jacob Perkins. By the 1850s refrigerated ships were carrying frozen meat across the oceans.

Frozen foods for the home were the brainwave of Clarence Birdseye. While fishing in a frozen lake, he saw that his catch was freezing hard on the ice. So why not freeze fresh fish and sell it?

Frozen foods soon caught on. The faster food is frozen, the better the taste, and the longer it keeps. Freezing kills the bacteria which cause decay.

▼WHEN WERE THE FIRST NEWSPAPERS PUBLISHED?

People began reading newspapers in the 1600s. Until then, news had traveled slowly by word of mouth.

In the Middle Ages, news of a foreign war, or the king's death, often took days to reach distant parts of the country. Town criers shouted out the news to townsfolk.

In the 1500s, after the invention of printing machinery, people began reading pamphlets and newsletters. The first newspaper to be printed regularly was called the *Corante*. It came out in London in 1621 and contained news from France, Italy, Spain and other countries.

Newspapers quickly became popular. In 1643 the first paper with pictures appeared. Its title was the *Civic Mercury*. By the 1700s, newspapers carried news of world events, business, shipping, farm prices, theater and gossip. Some of today's famous daily newspapers, such as *The Times*, began at this time.

▶WHEN DID THE FIRST ALPHABET APPEAR?

Stone Age people wrote in pictures. The first alphabet, with letters standing for sounds, appeared about 3,500 years ago.

In simple picture writing, a sign stands for an object – for example a bird. In time, picture writing also came to stand for ideas, so a bird sign might mean "flying." The people of ancient Egypt wrote in picture signs called hieroglyphics.

To write in picture signs, you need thousands of different pictures or characters. If signs stand for sounds, instead of things, it is easy to group them together to make words.

The Phoenicians, living in the eastern Mediterranean some 3,500 years ago, were the first to invent an alphabet of sound signs. Their alphabet was borrowed and improved by first the Greeks and then the Romans. Our word "alphabet" comes from the Greek words for the first two letters in their alphabet, *alpha* and *beta*.

PHOENICIAN	ANCIENT GREEK	MODERN ENGLISH
K ⅄	A	A
9 ⅁	B	B
1	Γ	C G
◁ ⅂	Δ	D
⅂ ⅂	E	E
Y	F	F
⊏ ⊏	Z	Z
Ħ H	H	H
⊗	Θ	
Ƨ	I	I J
Ⴟ ⅄	K	K
Ϛ L	Λ	L
ᄼ ᄽ	M	M
Ϡ ᄼ	N	N
⅄ ⅄	Ξ	X
Ŧ Ŧ Ʒ	O	O
O O	Π	P
1 ꒿	𝝨	Q
⅃Ꮧ ᄼ	Q	R
φφ φ	P Σ	S
ꓘ	T ϒ	T
W	Φ	U V
X	X Ψ	W
	Ω	Y

◀WHEN WAS INK FIRST MADE?

Writing was first done not with a pen and ink, but with a stick, making marks in wet clay. Writing on paper with ink began some 4,500 years ago.

The ancient Chinese and Egyptians used ink. They mixed soot or lampblack with gum to make a hard stick. The ink stick was mixed with water before being used. To make different colored inks, the Chinese and Egyptians used minerals, berries, plant juices and crushed insects.

The Chinese used brushes to write in ink and were the first to print with ink, using wooden blocks. When Gutenberg began printing in Europe in the 1400s, the ink was made by mixing varnish or boiled linseed oil with lampblack.

Quick-drying inks appeared in the 1700s. Today most printing inks are made by chemical processes. Different kinds of ink are used to print on cloth, plastic, paper and other materials.

▲WHEN WERE THE FIRST BANKS OPENED?

The first bankers were goldsmiths in the Middle Ages. But borrowing and lending money has been part of human affairs for much longer.

Ever since coins first appeared, some 2,500 years ago, people have traded in money. The word "bank" comes from the Italian *banco*, meaning "bench." Money changers and merchants did business from benches in the market place.

Goldsmiths looked after their gold in strong rooms. They let other people store their money there for safety. The paper receipts that the goldsmiths gave their customers came to be used as money – just like coins.

The bankers of Europe helped explorers and merchant adventurers by lending them money to buy ships and trade goods. The first big national bank was the Bank of England, which was started in 1694. The Bank of France began under Napoleon in 1800.

◄WHEN WERE BANK NOTES FIRST USED?

Coins and other forms of money had been in use for hundreds of years before bank notes appeared. China was the first to print paper money. Notes were not used in Europe until the 1600s.

Shells, stones, beads, teeth, even cattle, were used as money in ancient times. The first proper coins were made from gold and silver. The Greeks were the first people to issue coins that were checked for weight. These looked much the same as the coins we carry today. Modern coins, however, are made of cheaper metals than gold and silver.

Paper money came later, first in China, and then in Europe during the 1600s. The first European bank notes were issued by the Bank of Stockholm in Sweden in 1661. Paper money was lighter to carry than gold coins.

At first many people did not trust the new notes. In time they realized that a bank note was just as valuable as the sum in gold that it represented.

▶WHEN WERE POSTAGE STAMPS FIRST USED?

The ancient Chinese had a kind of postal system for sending messages. But postage stamps came into use only in 1840. Stamps made it easier and cheaper for people to send letters.

By the 1700s most European countries had some sort of postal service. In the U.S. too there were thousands of post offices by the 1830s. Letters were carried on horseback and by stagecoach.

In Britain, Rowland Hill saw that it would save time and money if letters could be sent any distance for a fixed charge. The simplest method was for the sender to buy a postage stamp and stick it on the letter. In 1840 the "penny post" was used for the first time.

Soon countries all over the world were issuing stamps. Most people could afford to post a letter, and it was not long before people also began to collect the stamps themselves. The development of railroads greatly speeded up the sending of mail.

◀ WHEN WERE FLAGS FIRST USED?

Battles are usually noisy and confused. Flags were used in ancient times to help soldiers keep in touch with their leaders. They could be seen amid the battle's confusion. Flags were also used to send signals.

Flags can be different shapes apart from the familiar rectangle most often seen today. A banner is a square flag; a standard has a long, streaming tail; and a gonfalon hangs down from a wooden cross bar.

In the Middle Ages every prince and nobleman had his own flag. In battle, the flag was held high to show everyone where their leader was. Medieval knights wore heraldic devices on their armor and shields to identify themselves. The devices usually appeared on their personal flags as well.

Today each country has its own national flag with special colors and designs. An example is the red, white and blue tricolor of France.

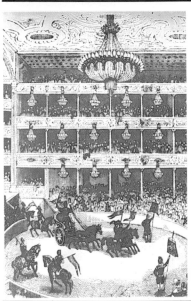

◀ WHEN DID MODERN CIRCUSES FIRST APPEAR?

In ancient Rome, the circus was a kind of stadium. In the 1700s the word "circus" was taken up by showmen for an exciting display of horsemanship.

In the Roman circus, there were chariot races and fights between wild animals and gladiators. In the 1770s, at the Royal Amphitheatre in London, a showman called Philip Astley staged thrilling displays of trick riding on horseback. This was the start of the modern circus.

Astley took his circus to France, and by 1790 similar shows had started in the U.S. As well as horses, performing animals and acrobats were to be seen. It was in the U.S. in the late 1800s that P. T. Barnum staged his famous three-ring circus, hailed as the "Greatest Show on Earth." One of its star attractions was a Wild West show, in which Buffalo Bill Cody and Indians took part. Barnum's circus traveled the world.

▶ WHEN WERE ANIMALS FIRST KEPT IN ZOOS?

Wild animals have been kept in zoos since ancient times. The first zoos were owned by great princes, who gave one another wild beasts as gifts.

There was a zoo in China at least 3,000 years ago, and there were other ancient zoos in the Middle East. King Solomon had a zoo. Nebuchadnezzar, King of Babylon, kept lions and other wild animals.

A famous medieval zoo was the royal zoo kept at the Tower

of London. This was eventually to become London Zoo, when the Zoological Society of London was founded in 1826.
There was a menagerie, or zoo, in Paris as early as 1333. The first modern zoo which tried to study animals and keep them in suitable conditions was the Austrian imperial zoo in Vienna. It was founded in 1752.

▶ WHEN DID ADVERTISING BECOME WIDESPREAD?

Advertising tells people about goods and services for sale. It is as old as trade itself. But advertising really caught on in the 1800s, when everyone began to read newspapers.

The Romans had shop signs. They also wrote graffiti on walls, with slogans such as "Vote for Marcus Perfidius." Advertising as we know it, however, had to wait until printed newspapers and magazines appeared.

In the 1600s English weekly papers carried advertisements for the new drinks, tea and coffee. By the 1700s most newspapers carried advertisements, and by the 1900s posters and slogans for products could be seen everywhere.

Radio advertising began in the U.S. in the 1920s, followed in the 1940s by television "commercials." Today advertising is common in the West, but it is less obvious in Communist countries.

▶ WHEN WERE CHRISTMAS CARDS INTRODUCED?

Christmas is a time of giving and receiving cards and presents. The first Christmas card was made in 1843. In a few years, the idea had caught on.

Sir Henry Cole, an Englishman, thought it would be nice to send a greetings card to his friends at Christmas. He asked a friend who was an artist to design one. On it was a picture of people eating and drinking cheerfully. Its message wished the receiver of the card a Merry Christmas and a Happy New Year.

In the 1840s the postal service was only just beginning. But by the 1880s so many people were sending Christmas cards that the post office had to ask them to "post early" to avoid delay. By then cheap printed cards were being sold in the thousands, although many people still made their own. Popular cards had pictures of angels, children, snowy scenes and flowers.

◀ WHEN WERE THE FIRST MOTION PICTURE FILMS MADE?

Photography was an invention of the 1800s. By the end of that century, audiences were enjoying moving pictures, with the coming of the movies.

Several people had the idea of showing still photgraphs on a screen very quickly, so that the figures in them appeared to move. Thomas Edison made his Kinetoscope, the first movie projector, in 1891. It used celluloid film, just as in a modern cinema.

In 1896 two French brothers, called Lumière (seen here), gave the first public film shows in Paris and London. The films were very short, lasting less than a minute, but people marveled all the same.

Soon film makers were putting stories on the screen. Georges Méliès of France began making movies in 1901. By 1915 motion picutres had advanced so much that D. W. Griffith could make epics such as *The Birth of a Nation*. The first films were silent.

TRANSPORTATION

▶ WHEN WAS THE STEAM LOCOMOTIVE INVENTED?

The steam engine was invented in the 1700s. It was used to drive pumps. Then a clever engineer saw that the power of steam could be used to turn wheels, to make a "locomotive."

Richard Trevithick, a Cornish mining engineer, built a "horseless carriage" driven by a steam engine in 1801. It ran on the roads. Later, in 1804, he made another, which ran on metal rails.

George Stephenson and other engineers took up this idea. Stephenson built a steam locomotive for the first public railroad in 1825. In 1829 he won a competition for the best

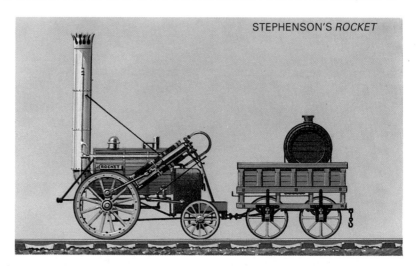

STEPHENSON'S *ROCKET*

engine with his locomotive "Rocket." This locomotive managed a top speed of 35 miles an hour. Its success started the railroad age, and its design was widely copied. The locomotive was driven by two cylinders powered by steam

from a multi-tube boiler.

In 1830 Stephenson's locomotives opened the Liverpool and Manchester Railway. This was the first public railroad meant from the start to be used only by steam trains.

▶ WHEN WAS THE FIRST PUBLIC RAILROAD OPENED?

The first public railroad in the world was the Stockton and Darlington line in northeast England. It opened in 1825, and its trains were hauled by the first steam railroad locomotive.

Railroads had been used to move coal for many years. But the wagons were horse-drawn. The invention of the steam locomotive brought a completely new form of transportation.

George Stephenson persuaded the owners of the Stockton and Darlington Railway to use his new steam

engine instead of horses. He drove the first train himself. The locomotive was called *Locomotion*, and the first passenger coach was called *Experiment*. It looked like a horse-drawn carriage, with

railroad wheels instead of coach wheels.

On the first trains, passengers often sat in open cars. Smoke and sparks from the locomotive's chimney made it an uncomfortable ride.

▼WHICH WAS THE FIRST TRANSCONTINENTAL RAILROAD?

In the 1800s settlers headed west across the vast new land of America. They dreamed of a railroad across the continent. In 1869 that dream came true.

Railroads began to be built in America soon after the start of the railroad age. The first public steam railroad in the U.S. was opened in 1830.

The first U.S. railroads were short, joining the towns of the eastern states. Crossing the Wild West was a far more difficult task. Work on the transcontinental railroad began in 1863. The Union Pacific headed west from Iowa, while the Central Pacific started laying track eastward from California.

The railroads had to cross rivers, deserts, mountains, swamps and ravines. Often hostile Indians fought to stop the "iron horse" from crossing their hunting grounds.

The photograph shows the two tracks meeting in Utah, in 1869. The completed railroad was 1,724 miles long. New towns sprang up alongside the tracks. Trains carried settlers west to California, and east to the big cities.

▲WHEN WERE DIESEL LOCOMOTIVES FIRST USED?

In 1932 the first diesel railroad locomotive went into service. Diesel trains quickly took over from steam trains after that.

The diesel engine was invented by the German engineer Rudolf Diesel in 1894. It is a form of internal combustion engine which burns less fuel than other types of engine. In 1932 the German railroads started using diesel locomotives. By the 1950s diesels were common on other railroads, especially in the U.S.

The largest diesel locomotives haul heavy trains on the U.S. railroads. Often several engines are needed to pull one train. The diesel engine is usually connected to an electricity generator, which produces electric power to work the motors turning the wheels of the locomotive.

Diesel locomotives can reach speeds of over 125 miles an hour, but the world's fastest trains are electric (up to 205 miles an hour). Electric trains, which take current from the rails or overhead wires, are common. However, diesel still rules the rails in North America.

▲WHEN WAS THE FIRST AIRCRAFT FLIGHT MADE?

People flew in a balloon in 1783. It was not until 1903 that an airplane (a heavier-than-air flying machine) first flew. Yet within a few years, airplanes were crossing the oceans.

After the Montgolfier brothers proved that people could fly in balloons (1783), it seemed that the problems of flight had been solved. Unfortunately, balloons can only go where the wind takes them. People tried putting sails, oars and steam engines into balloons to beat this problem. They also tried airships and gliders.

On December 17, 1903, the long wait ended. Two Americans, Orville and Wilbur Wright, tested a gasoline-engined airplane called the *Flyer*. It took off and flew, with Orville as pilot, for 130 feet at Kitty Hawk in North Carolina.

▶WHEN WERE THE FIRST METAL PLANES BUILT?

Early planes were made of wood and canvas to keep down weight. Not until the 1930s did metal planes take to the skies.

Most of the planes that fought in World War I were biplanes (double-winged). They looked rather like box kites, with their wings held together by wooden struts and wires.

The monoplane has a single set of wings. It is better for high-speed flight because its shape is more streamlined (smooth). One of the first monoplane fighters was the Russian Polikarpov 1-16 of 1933.

The German designer Hugo Junkers began building all-metal airplanes, the most famous of which was the Junkers Ju-52 (1932). The new metal planes had bodies shaped like smooth tapering tubes. Light but strong alloys (mixtures of metals) were used to build them. Today almost all airplanes are built of metal, specially made to withstand the heat and stress of high speeds.

JUNKERS JU-52

▲WHEN DID THE FIRST AIRLINERS FLY?

Passenger air travel began after World War I. The airplanes were unwanted warplanes, slow and uncomfortable. But by the 1930s larger, faster and more comfortable airliners had appeared.

In the 1920s an air journey was often cold and bumpy. Long flights took days, for the plane had to land several times to refuel. The first "modern" airliner was the all-metal American Boeing 247 of 1933. It carried ten passengers.

One of the largest 1930s airliners, however, was an old-fashioned biplane, the HP 42. This British airliner flew slowly, but comfortably, from London to Africa and India. Another famous airliner was the Douglas DC-3 of the 1940s. It carried 21 passengers.

Flying boats were also popular in the 1930s. They crossed the great oceans, landing on the water rather than on concrete runways.

▶WHEN DID THE FIRST JETS FLY?

The fastest a propeller-driven plane can fly is around 470 miles an hour. In 1939 a new age of speed began, with the first flight by a jet plane.

A British engineer named Frank Whittle had worked on the theory of jet flight since the early 1930s. He wanted to build an engine which, because it needed no propeller, would work well in the thin air at great heights.

GLOSTER-WHITTLE E28/39

Germany was also at work on the jet engine. In 1939 the Heinkel He 179 made the world's first jet flight. The Germans also built the first jet warplane, the Me 262. It was a twin-jet fighter-bomber.

Whittle's own engine was first flown in 1941. The plane was the Gloster E28/39. Jets came too late to play much part in World War II.

CONCORDE

FW-61 HELICOPTER

▲WHEN WERE HELICOPTERS INVENTED?

Inventors drew plans for flying machines very like helicopters in the 1400s. But it was not until 1936 that the first practical helicopter took to the air.

A helicopter has no wings. It lifts itself off the ground by means of a large rotor, or propeller. Once aloft, the rotor is tilted slightly forward to make the helicopter fly forward. Helicopters can fly backward too, and even hover

in one spot in midair.

The famous Italian artist and inventor Leonardo da Vinci drew a helicopter. But his machine never flew. The first successful helicopter was the German FW-61 of 1936. It had two rotors. A Russian, Igor Sikorsky, did much to advance helicopter design, and Sikorsky helicopters were used during World War II. After the war, the use of helicopters increased enormously.

◀WHICH WAS THE FIRST SUPERSONIC AIRLINER?

Aircraft first broke the "sound barrier" in the 1940s. Today the *Concorde* carries passengers at over twice the speed of sound.

At sea level, sound travels at about 746 miles an hour. Higher up, the speed is slower, around 590 miles an hour. When a plane reaches this speed, it makes a shock wave in the air. This wave can be heard as a "sonic boom."

Only a jet or rocket plane can reach such high speeds. The American Bell X-1 was the first piloted plane to break the "sound barrier" and prove that supersonic flight was not really dangerous.

In the 1960s two supersonic airliners were built. The Russian Tupolev Tu-144 first flew in 1968, but did not prove a success. The *Concorde*, built by Britain and France, flew a year later and went into regular airline service in 1976. The *Concorde* is smaller than a jumbo jet, but much faster, crossing the Atlantic at over 1,240 miles an hour.

▶WHEN WERE THE FIRST SHIPS BUILT?

People probably used logs to float across rivers. These were the first boats. Ships large enough to sail the open sea were first made in Egypt 5,000 years ago.

Logs tied together made a raft. A log hollowed out made a canoe. Reeds tied in bundles would also float. We know that the ancient Egyptians made reed boats, because pictures of them have been found in tombs. But such craft (shown in the picture) were only safe for river travel.

The Egyptians made larger boats, with sails and oars, to explore the open sea. Other peoples living on the shores of the Mediterranean Sea also built boats. They built long, slender galleys for war and broad, slower-moving cargo ships for trade. Oars were used to drive the ship along when there was not enough wind.

The sailors kept in sight of land. They had no maps or compasses to navigate with.

▶WHEN WERE FULL-RIGGED SHIPS USED?

Most early ships had one large sail. By the 1400s ships had three masts carrying several sails. These were the first "full-rigged" ships.

CARRACK

A ship's rig is its arrangement of sails. The first seagoing vessels usually had a single square sail, although some had a triangular or "lateen" sail instead.

As ships grew larger, extra sails were added. Square and triangular sails were found to work well together. By the 1400s the three-masted carrack had appeared. This was the first full-rigged ship. It was steered by a stern rudder, replacing the older steering oar.

After the carrack came the galleon. As ship design improved, extra sails were added for greater speed. By the 1800s the fastest clippers could sail at 24 miles an hour (21 knots).

▶WHEN WERE SUBMARINES FIRST BUILT?

Since ancient times, sailors have dreamed of traveling beneath the sea. But not until 1801 did an inventor make a submarine craft. It took years to develop the submarines of today.

Amazingly, a kind of submarine was tried as early as 1620, though it was little more than a watertight barrel. In 1775 an American one-man submarine called *Turtle* tried to sink a British warship. But the honor of building the first submarine goes to Robert Fulton of the U.S., whose Nautilus of 1801 could stay under water for four hours.

However, it was not until the 1890s that navies finally accepted submarines, thanks to the work of another American, John Holland. His submarine set the model for the craft used in World Wars I and II. It had gasoline engines for surface travel and electric motors for moving beneath the waves.

TURTLE SUBMARINE

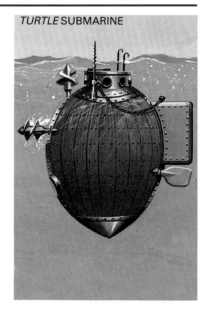

▲ WHEN WERE THE GREAT DAYS OF SAILING SHIPS?

For thousands of years sailing ships ruled the seas. Their greatest days came in the 1700s and early 1800s. This was the age of the great wooden battleships and the graceful China clippers.

By the 1500s the shape of the sailing ship had become settled. For the next 300 years it did not change very much. However, there were many improvements.

The greatest warships of the days of sail were 100-gun and 74-gun battleships. These wooden ships had cannon ranged along their sides. In battle, they sailed alongside one another, firing broadsides of cannon balls. Ships like these fought at the battle of Trafalgar in 1805.

In the 1840s came the last and most elegant of all sailing ships – the clipper (shown in the picture). Its task was to carry tea from China to the U.S. and Britain. It was built for speed, and could sail 400 miles in a day. To reach port first (and so get the highest prices for their cargo), the tea clippers sometimes raced one another across the oceans. As well as tea, clippers also carried wool from Australia.

Although fast, the clippers (like all sailing ships) relied on favorable winds. In time, these graceful ships gave way to the steamship, which could keep up the same speed, day and night, whatever the wind.

CLERMONT

▲ WHEN DID THE FIRST STEAMSHIPS SAIL?

Just as sailing ships reached their peak, they were challenged by a new rival – the steamer. The first steamships took to the seas in the early 1800s. Soon they ruled the waves.

A steam-powered river boat called the *Pyroscaphe* was built in France in 1783. But the first practical steamboats were the U.S. *Clermont* of 1807 and the Scottish *Comet* of 1812. Both had steam engines driving paddle wheels.

In 1819 a small steamer called *Savannah* sailed across the Atlantic, although it only used its engine for part of the way.

In the 1840s the screw propeller began to replace the paddle wheel on steamships. I. K. Brunel's steamship *Great Eastern* (1858) had both screws and paddles. It was built to sail all the way to Australia without taking on extra coal for its boilers.

▶WHEN WAS THE INTERNAL COMBUSTION ENGINE INVENTED?

The internal combustion engine burns gasoline as fuel. It is light but powerful. The first such engine appeared in 1876.

A German engineer called Nikolaus Otto had been experimenting with "gas engines" since the 1860s. So too had other inventors. In 1876 Otto built the first gasoline engine that worked well. It was a four-stroke engine, in which burning gasoline forced a piston up and down a cylinder.

This up-and-down motion could be carried through belts, chains or rods to turn wheels. So the gasoline engine could be used to drive a wheeled vehicle.

Otto's assistant was Gottlieb Daimler, who fitted a gasoline engine to a tricycle in 1886. Another German, Carl Benz, built a single-cylinder engine which drove a three-wheeled car at nine miles an hour in 1885. These two machines were the forerunners of the modern automobile.

The internal combustion engine had many advantages over the older steam engine. It was smaller, lighter and quieter. So it became the standard engine for use in automobiles and motor cycles.

In the gasoline engine, the gas is burned by an electric spark. In the diesel engine, compressed air gives the heat needed to light the gas. The diesel engine is named after its inventor, Rudolf Diesel of Germany, who built the first one in 1894.

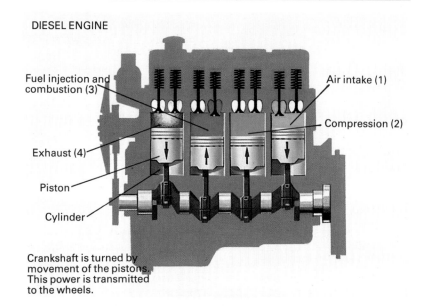

DIESEL ENGINE

Fuel injection and combustion (3)
Air intake (1)
Compression (2)
Exhaust (4)
Piston
Cylinder

Crankshaft is turned by movement of the pistons. This power is transmitted to the wheels.

BENZ *VELO*

▲WHEN WAS THE FIRST MOTOR CAR BUILT?

The first cars were known as "horseless carriages." They took to the roads in the 1880s. It was the gasoline engine that made possible the age of the automobile.

In 1770 Nicolas Cugnot, a French inventor, built a steam tractor. It was the world's first powered vehicle, but it was very slow. Although other steam cars were built, steam engines were not really suitable for road transport.

During the 1860s the problems of making a reliable gasoline engine were solved. In 1886 Gottlieb Daimler of Germany made the first car fitted with a gasoline engine.

By 1893 cars such as the Benz Velo were being built and sold to enthusiastic motorists in Europe and America. Henry Ford built his first car in 1896 and went on to start the world's first car factory. He used the production line system to make cars quickly and cheaply.

▼WHEN WERE MOTOR-CYCLES FIRST PRODUCED?

In the early days of motoring, there was little difference between motor cars and motor bicycles. The first machine to be called a "motor-cycle" was made in 1893.

In the 1860s people tried fitting steam engines to tricycles, but the machines were slow and heavy. Gottlieb Daimler in Germany and Edward Butler in Britain experimented with gasoline-engined cycles in the 1880s.

In 1893 Hildebrand and Wolfmuller of Germany built a motorcycle which could do 23 miles an hour. Cycles with motors quickly became popular. In 1895 de Dion and Bouton of France built a motor-cycle with a small, lightweight gasoline engine. Most other early motor cycles were based on this machine. In many ways, it helped decide the shape of the automobile, as well as the motor cycle. Motor-cycle racing began in the early 1900s.

HILDEBRAND & WOLFMULLER MOTOR CYCLE

▲WHEN WERE THE FIRST RACING CARS BUILT?

Soon after the first motor cars appeared on the roads, people began racing them. Road races started in the 1890s. Grand Prix ("Chief Prize") racing began in 1906.

The first races were held on ordinary roads. They were tests of endurance rather than speed, and the first racing cars were much the same as the models sold to the public.

As cars got faster, accidents became common, and in 1903 road races were banned. Instead, cars raced on special tracks. Today there is a huge difference between Grand Prix racers and ordinary family cars.

The first Grand Prix was the French. The first race took place in 1906, near Le Mans. The drivers had to complete 12 laps in two days round a 103-kilometer course. Only 11 of the 32 starters finished the race. After World War I other countries started their own Grand Prix races.

▼WHEN DID BUSES FIRST APPEAR ON THE ROADS?

In medieval times, few people traveled far from home. But in the 1800s, as towns grew larger, people needed a cheap form of transportation. The bus was the answer.

In the 1700s travelers on a long journey faced days of discomfort inside a bumpy stagecoach pulled by horses. By the 1800s railroads had replaced the coach for long journeys. For short distances, horse-drawn buses had taken to the roads.

Horse buses ran in the streets from the 1820s. Instead of walking to work, people could now ride. Soon afterward came the streetcar, a bus running on rails through the streets.

Horse-drawn buses were used until the early 1900s. Then motor buses took over. Electric streetcars ran in city streets until more recently. Then, as the roads grew busier with cars, it was decided that streetcar lines were a nuisance. So they were abolished in many of the world's cities.

PLANET EARTH

▶WHEN WAS THE EARTH FORMED?

The oldest rocks found so far are thought to be about 3.85 billion years old – so the earth had a solid crust by then. Some meteorites and pieces of moon rock are probably 4.6 billion years old, so scientists now think that the earth and other parts of our solar system were formed about 4.6 billion years ago.

As scientists have studied the earth's rocks more, they have decided on an earlier and earlier date for the earth's formation. In the 17th century, Archbishop Ussher dated the earth's creation to 4004 B.C. By the 19th century, geologists thought the earth might be 100 million years old. During this century, scientists have discovered that many rocks contain radioactive elements which gradually decay over long periods of time. With special equipment, the rate of decay can be measured.

Early attempts to measure the age of the earth with the help of radioactive elements in rocks put its formation at two billion years ago. Today scientists believe it is more than twice as old. They base their estimates on tests made on samples of very old rocks from remote areas such as Greenland, and also on moon rock and meteorites.

▶WHEN WAS THE SAHARA DESERT COVERED BY ICE?

Geologists have found evidence of glaciation in the bedrock of the Algerian desert. This suggests that the Sahara was covered by ice about 450 million years ago. Further studies suggest that when this happened the area was situated near the South Pole.

The shape and position of the continents on our globe have not always been the same. The earth's crust is broken into many giant "plates," which are slowly moving. As they move, they carry the continents with them. Some plates contain whole continents, such as Australia. Some plates contain parts of the present continents.

About 200 million years ago, in Triassic times, there was one supercontinent called Pangaea. This has since broken apart. Pangaea was formed when separate continental plates drifted together.

The history of the continents before the formation of Pangaea is still rather uncertain. But evidence from rocks, especially rock magnetism, shows that 450 million years ago, in Ordovician times, today's Sahara lay at the South Pole. The Equator ran diagonally across today's North America.

▶WHEN DID THE OLD WORLD AND THE NEW WORLD SEPARATE?

The continents of the Old World (Europe, Asia and Africa) and the New World (North and South America) have been slowly drifting on the surface of the earth since our planet became solid. About 200 million years ago they were joined together in Pangaea. Then the Atlantic opened up, separating the Americas from Africa and Europe. The Americas drifted westward to join Asia for a time.

Since Jurassic times, the Atlantic Ocean has opened up very slowly. In the last 150 million years, it has changed from a broad rift valley to a wide ocean. Samples of rocks and sediments from the ocean floor enable geologists to date the different parts of the Atlantic and work out the average rate of movement of the continents.

The South Atlantic formed first, as the southern continents split apart. Then North America separated from Europe and drifted toward eastern Asia. Land which now forms both Alaska in North America and the Chukchi Peninsula of Siberia joined on to the rest of Siberia.

During the Pleistocene Ice Ages there were many changes of sea level, forming the Bering Strait. At present, Alaska and Siberia are separated by this narrow, shallow sea.

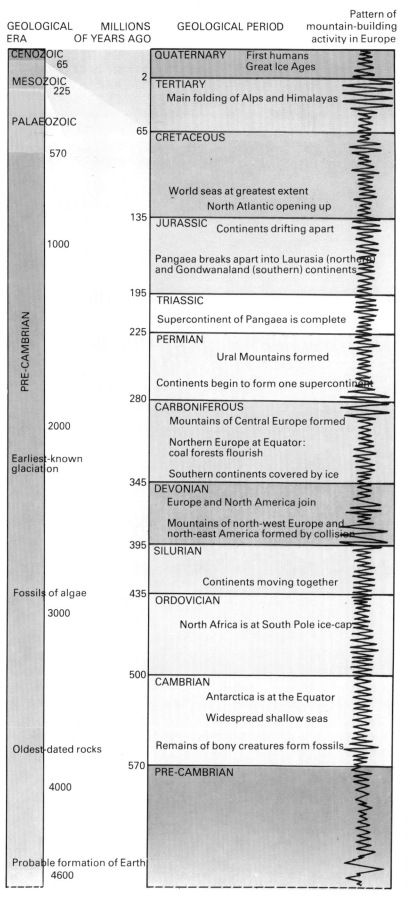

GEOLOGICAL ERA	MILLIONS OF YEARS AGO	GEOLOGICAL PERIOD	Pattern of mountain-building activity in Europe
CENOZOIC	65	QUATERNARY — First humans, Great Ice Ages	
MESOZOIC	2	TERTIARY — Main folding of Alps and Himalayas	
	225		
PALAEOZOIC	65	CRETACEOUS	
	570	World seas at greatest extent	
		North Atlantic opening up	
	135	JURASSIC — Continents drifting apart	
	1000	Pangaea breaks apart into Laurasia (northern) and Gondwanaland (southern) continents	
	195	TRIASSIC — Supercontinent of Pangaea is complete	
	225	PERMIAN — Ural Mountains formed	
		Continents begin to form one supercontinent	
	280	CARBONIFEROUS — Mountains of Central Europe formed	
	2000	Northern Europe at Equator: coal forests flourish	
		Southern continents covered by ice	
	345	DEVONIAN — Europe and North America join	
		Mountains of north-west Europe and north-east America formed by collision	
	395	SILURIAN — Continents moving together	
	3000	ORDOVICIAN	
	435	North Africa is at South Pole ice-cap	
	500	CAMBRIAN — Antarctica is at the Equator	
		Widespread shallow seas	
		Remains of bony creatures form fossils	
	570	PRE-CAMBRIAN	
	4000		
	4600	Probable formation of Earth	

Left margin labels: PRE-CAMBRIAN; Earliest-known glaciation; Fossils of algae; Oldest-dated rocks; Probable formation of Earth

◄WHEN DID THE ALPS FORM?

The Alps are made mainly of rock layers which were uplifted and folded about 25 million years ago.

The Alps are part of a series of fold mountains stretching through southern Europe and the Middle East to the Himalayas and other mountains of Asia. They are the result of the movement of the continents.

Africa and Asia drifted eastward and rotated toward each other. Sediments in the ocean floor between these continents were compressed, folded, faulted and uplifted. About 25 million years ago these movements speeded up. The uplift was much faster than erosion, so great mountains formed.

◄WHEN WAS THE MEDITERRANEAN SEA DRY?

Six million years ago the Mediterranean Sea was a dry valley. Boreholes made in many places beneath the present sea have revealed a layer of salt hundreds of feet thick.

The climate around the present Mediterranean must have been much hotter and drier in Tertiary times, about six million years ago. Few rivers flowed, and water must have evaporated quickly. A mountain range across the Strait of Gibraltar kept out the waters of the Atlantic Ocean. Geologists think that this mountain dam was breached about five and a half million years ago. Salt water poured in, flooding the present Mediterranean.

▼WHEN DID PEOPLE DISCOVER THAT THE EARTH IS ROUND?

The ancient Greeks discovered that the earth is round. Pythagoras (582–507 B.C.) described the earth as a sphere.

The Greeks studied the shadow of the earth and moon during eclipses. They believed a sphere to be the perfect shape, so thought that all heavenly bodies, and the universe itself, must be spherical. In 350 B.C., Aristotle argued that the earth is round.

Although the Greeks were right about the earth's shape, most of them believed that it was at the center of the universe. About 280 B.C., Aristarchus said that the sun is at the center, but his ideas were ignored for 1,500 years.

When the Roman Empire broke up, Greek ideas were condemned by the Church or forgotten. But the Arabs kept Greek ideas alive through their translations, and later medieval scholars and map makers rediscovered that the earth is round.

▼WHEN DID SEA CHARTS COME INTO USE?

The earliest record of a sea-chart dates from 1270, when Louis IX of France studied a chart on board a Genoan ship during the Eighth Crusade.

The earliest navigators kept close to land or drifted with ocean currents. Once the compass was used, ships could sail more directly from one port to another. The Chinese and Arabs may have used sea charts before Europeans, but none survive.

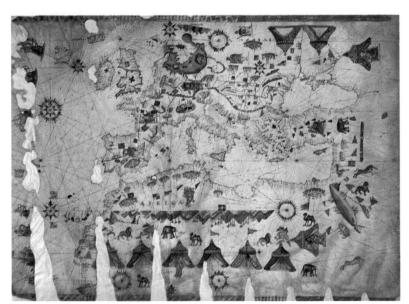

◄WHEN WERE THE FIRST MAPS MADE?

Simple sketch maps were probably drawn before people could write, so maps may be older than written history. The oldest surviving map was drawn on a Babylonian clay tablet about 2300 B.C.

An ancient map was found at Gar-Sur, nearly 250 miles north of Babylon. It shows mountains and a river (probably the Euphrates) flowing through a delta.

The ancient Egyptians drew

From about 1200, compasses and rudders were used on European ships. Navigators used *portolani* – books which listed ports, landmarks, distances and navigation advice. Later, charts were added to these books. The Genoans were great sailors and compiled the oldest-known *portolani* and charts. Other countries copied them. By 1354 sea charts were more common. The chart shown here dates from 1548. It shows the Mediterranean and part of the Atlantic.

maps to record land boundaries. But scientific map making began with the ancient Greeks who worked out the size and shape of the earth.

The Greek geographer Claudius Ptolemy, shown here, drew maps of the whole world. In his famous work *Geographia*, he discussed globes, map projections and principles of map making. Arab geographers translated Ptolemy's writings, and in 1405 a Latin translation was made. For several centuries many new maps were based on this.

**The first aerial photographs
were taken from a balloon
above Paris in 1858. The
photographer and balloonist
was Gaspard Felix
Tournachon, who was also
known as Nadar.**

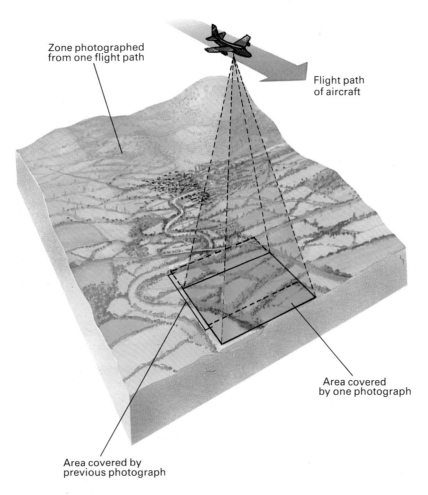

Zone photographed
from one flight path

Flight path
of aircraft

Area covered
by one photograph

Area covered by
previous photograph

These first air photographs of
Paris were used to help with
map making. Experiments
continued with balloons and
kites, but it was not until
World War I that aerial
photography became really
useful for reconnaisance
mapping. As better lenses,
cameras and planes were made
after 1918, many more air
photographs were taken.
During World War II, vast
areas of the world were
mapped from air photographs.

Modern air photographs are
taken with a 60 percent
overlap, as shown in the
diagram. When pairs of
photographs are viewed
stereoscopically, the land
appears in 3-D and contours
can be plotted. Satellites are
also used for aerial
photography.

▶WHEN WAS THE FIRST
ATLAS PRODUCED?

**The first collection of maps
to be called an atlas was
published by Gerardus
Mercator in 1585. The
picture shows the title page
from one of these books.**

Until printing was invented,
maps were handmade and very
expensive. In 1477, a Latin
version of Ptolemy's
Geographia was printed.

Abraham Ortelius of
Antwerp produced the first
modern type of atlas in 1570. It

had 70 maps. At the same
time, Gerardus Mercator was
working on a series of volumes
in which he planned to
describe the creation and
history of the world. He
named it after the Greek god
Atlas because he symbolized
the study of heaven and earth.

Part one of Mercator's atlas
was a list of important dates
and events up to the year 1568.
The maps were not published
until 1585. They included
world maps drawn on a map-
projection which is still named
after Mercator.

▼WHEN DID CROP ROTATION BEGIN IN EUROPE?

All crops take goodness out of the soil, but some crops are able to put goodness back into it. Farmers can improve their soil with manures and fertilizers; by resting the soil for a fallow year; and by growing different kinds of crops after each other in the same fields.

Variations of the medieval three-field system (top diagram) have been used in Europe for over 2,000 years. In the three-field system, large fields are divided into strips which are cultivated by different farmers. Every year, two fields are cultivated and the third is left fallow. Today, modern fertilizers make a fallow year unnecessary.

A new system which cut out the fallow year was probably first used in the Netherlands in the 15th century. Fodder crops were grown on the land, instead of using a fallow year. In this way, farmers could cultivate all the land all the time, though they did not then know that many fodder crops put nitrogen back into the soil. Plants need nitrogen to grow properly.

In 17th-century England, pioneers of new farming methods introduced the Norfolk four-course rotation (lower diagram). In this system, cereal crops such as wheat and barley alternate with clover and root crops. Cereal crops take a lot of goodness out of the soil, but clover puts nitrogen back into the soil. Even with modern fertilizers, farmers still use crop rotation.

THREE-FIELD SYSTEM

Fallow (no crops)

Cereal crops (wheat or rye)

Other crops (barley, oats or peas)

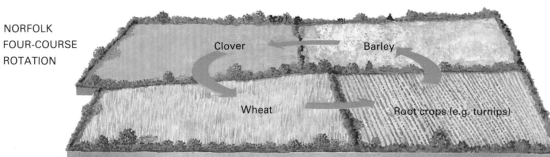

NORFOLK FOUR-COURSE ROTATION

Clover

Barley

Wheat

Root crops (e.g. turnips)

Sugar beet   Sugar cane

◄WHEN WAS SUGAR INTRODUCED TO EUROPE?

The sugar we eat is refined from either sugar cane (a tropical grass) or sugar beet (a temperate root crop).

Sugar making may have started in India about 3000 B.C. Alexander the Great took samples home to Greece.

The Arabs learned about sugar making from India. By the 8th century, Arabs were growing cane and making sugar in Spain and France.

Christopher Columbus took sugar cane from Europe to the West Indies in 1493. Gradually, sugar plantations were established in many parts of the New World. The sugar trade across the Atlantic became very important.

At the beginning of the 19th century, Europe could not get sugar supplies from America because of the Napoleonic Wars. By then, a few people had proved that sugar could be obtained from certain kinds of beet. Napoleon encouraged the growth and refining of beet sugar in Europe.

►WHEN DID THE GREEN REVOLUTION TAKE PLACE?

The Green Revolution is the spread of modern ideas in agriculture, using better seeds, fertilizers and irrigation to grow more food.

The story of the Green Revolution began in the 1950s when scientists began to increase wheat production in Mexico. Soon, research institutes were set up in Mexico, Colombia, Nigeria and the Philippines. Seeds of high-yielding varieties of wheat, corn and rice were sent to farmers round the world. These began to increase food production in the late 1960s. In 1970, Dr. Norman Borlaug received the Nobel Peace Prize for his work on the Green Revolution.

The Green Revolution has its own problems, however. The new crops need regular supplies of fertilizer and water, which are not always available. Diseases attack the new plants, and in many places only the richest farmers can afford the new seeds.

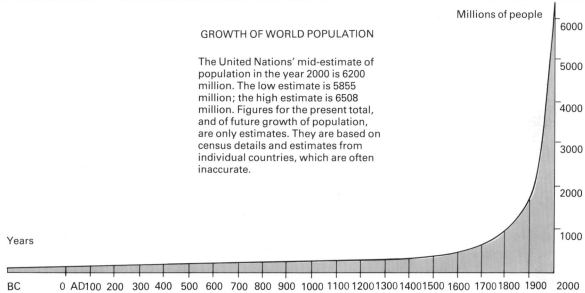

GROWTH OF WORLD POPULATION

The United Nations' mid-estimate of population in the year 2000 is 6200 million. The low estimate is 5855 million; the high estimate is 6508 million. Figures for the present total, and of future growth of population, are only estimates. They are based on census details and estimates from individual countries, which are often inaccurate.

Millions of people

Years

▲WHEN WILL THE WORLD'S POPULATION DOUBLE?

At present, the world's population is estimated to be nearly 4.6 billion people. If the present rate of population growth continues, this figure will double in 40 years.

The world's population reached one billion people by about 1830. Only 100 years later, it reached two billion people. In 50 years, the figure doubled again, and the next doubling could be in only 40 years. No wonder we hear of the "population explosion."

Population growth occurs when the number of babies born is greater than the number of deaths. On average, parents are having fewer children now than in past years, but the population has "exploded" because the death rate has declined. As killer dieases are conquered, and health care improves, more babies survive and grow up to have children of their own. More adults also live to old age. The rate of population growth varies in different parts of the world. In most of Western Europe, it will take at least 400 years for the population to double. But the population of Africa may double in 24 years.

In most countries where population growth is rapid at present, governments are discouraging large families. China now has a "one child only" policy. If people feel secure enough to limit the size of their families, or if simpler methods of birth control are found, the doubling time of the earth's population may be stretched by peaceful means.

OUT IN SPACE

▼ WHEN WERE THE FIRST ASTRONOMICAL OBSERVATIONS MADE?

People began observing the sky many thousands of years ago. The oldest surviving observational records may be 3,500 years old.

One of the oldest surviving structures in the world, the Great Pyramid in Egypt, was built about 4,500 years ago. It seems to have been lined up with the position of one or more bright stars in the sky. About 500 years later, Stonehenge in England could have been used to indicate the midsummer sunrise position.

The ancient Chinese recorded information by carving on animal bones. Scholars think that one of these refers to an astronomical observation made about 3,500 years ago.

▼ WHEN WERE THE FIRST OBSERVATORIES BUILT?

The first "observatories" were built long before telescopes were invented. The building shown here may have been an obervatory. It was built by the Toltec people of Mexico around the 13th century A.D.

A structure in Korea, dating from about A.D. 640, may have been an observatory. The most elaborate of ancient observatories was built in Persia some 600 years ago by Ulugh Begh, but we do not know what it looked like. The most important early observatory was built by the Danish astronomer Tycho Brahe four centuries ago. He made many important observations, even without a telescope.

▼ WHEN WAS HALLEY'S COMET FIRST SEEN?

Halley's Comet orbits the sun every 76 years or so. It is visible with the naked eye for only a few months as it passes nearest to the sun. It was observed as long ago as 240 B.C., and has been seen at every return since, except one: a total of 28 returns altogether.

Edmund Halley was the first person to realize that some of these historical sightings were all of the same object. He concluded that the comets seen in 1531, 1607 and 1682 were one and the same object. He therefore predicted that it would return again in 1758–59. It was seen on Christmas evening, 1758, proving beyond doubt that it was in orbit around the sun.

▼WHEN WERE THE CONSTELLATIONS FIRST NAMED?

The names of many constellations date back for thousands of years, having been observed by the ancient peoples of the Middle East. The names were passed on to us through the Greeks and Romans. Some well-known constellations, such as the Great Bear (Ursa Major), were mentioned in the *Odyssey*, **for example, over 2,000 years ago.**

Altogether, 88 different constellations are recognized over the whole sky today. Of these, 49 are ancient. They were known by their familiar names by the time the astronomer Ptolemy made his famous catalogue around A.D. 150. It is possible that shepherds and casual star-gazers saw pictures in the star patterns, and turned them into the figures we recognize today.

With the great sea voyages of the 17th century came an interest in the southern skies, which had not previously been observed. This is how the *modern* constellations came into existence. Some of their names sound very strange. For example, there is a furnace (Fornax) and a clock (Horologium) among this new group!

The pictures show an ancient constellation (Aquila, the Eagle) and a modern one (Scutum, the Shield). Often, the brightest star in a constellation has its own proper name, such as Altair in Aquila.

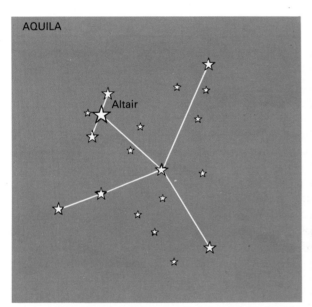

AQUILA
Altair

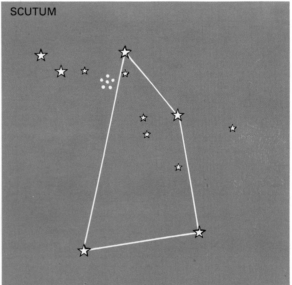

SCUTUM

►WHEN WERE THE FIRST TELESCOPES USED?

The telescope was invented in 1608 by a Dutchman, Hans Lippershey. Although lenses had been used in spectacles for many years, this was the first time that anyone worked out how to combine two lenses in a tube so as to give a close-up view of a distant object.

The Italian astronomer Galileo was one of the first people to turn a telescope to the sky, in 1609. Two of his instruments

are shown in the picture. These early telescopes did not give a very sharp image, and were not very large. Nevertheless, Galileo made many important discoveries, including the four bright satellites of Jupiter and the phases of Venus.

A hundred years later, reflecting telescopes (using mirrors instead of lenses) made their appearance. The first really successful reflecting telescope was made in 1721 by John Hadley in England.

Soviet spacecraft made the first direct landings. *Luna 2* **landed on the moon on September 13, 1959.** *Venera 3* **reached Venus on March 1, 1966, and** *Mars 2* **(shown here) landed on Mars on November 27, 1971. The first American craft to reach another world was** *Ranger 7*, **which struck the moon on July 31, 1964.**

These early achievements were all crash landings, each spacecraft being destroyed. The first successful "soft" landing on the moon was made by the Soviet craft *Luna 9* on February 3, 1966. It was followed by the American *Surveyor 1* on June 2, 1966.

Venera 4, which landed on Venus on October 18, 1967, was the first probe to send back information from the surface of another planet. The first successful landing on Mars was made by the American *Viking 1* on July 20, 1976, exactly seven years after the first men landed on the moon.

▲WHEN WAS THE FIRST ROCKET-PROPELLED VEHICLE LAUNCHED?

Rockets in the form of fireworks have been known for centuries, but the first flight of a true rocket vehicle took place on March 16, 1926. It was built and launched by an American, Robert Hutchings Goddard (shown here). His rocket rose about 200 feet into the air!

Goddard's rocket was fueled by gasoline and liquid oxygen. He was interested in exploring the upper atmosphere, but also realized that by using two or three *step rockets*, which fire in succession, it would be possible to escape into space.

On October 3, 1942, a rocket achieved an altitude of 62 miles. This happened in a test-firing of the famous V-2 rocket used by Germany in World War II. The first rocket to reach interplanetary space was a two-stage vehicle fired to a height of 250 miles from New Mexico in 1949.

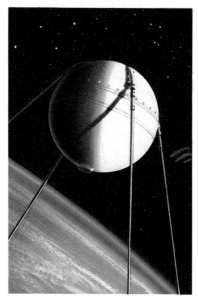

▲WHEN WAS THE FIRST ARTIFICIAL SATELLITE LAUNCHED?

On October 4, 1957, the Soviet Union launched *Sputnik 1* **into orbit around the earth. The launch pad was in central Asia. The Sputnik was a metal sphere about two feet across, and weighed about 180 pounds.**

Sputnik 1 orbited the earth once every 96 minutes at a height of about 125 miles. Its launch took American space scientists by surprise, for there had as yet been no attempt to launch a satellite.

U.S. experts made a rushed attempt at launching a satellite on December 6, but the rocket exploded on the launch pad. However, on January 31, 1958, the Americans put *Explorer 1* into orbit. It weighed only 30 pounds. This satellite swept further away from the earth in the course of its orbit, and sent back information which led to the discovery of the Van Allen belts of radiation around our planet.

▶WHEN DID THE FIRST MAN FLY IN SPACE?

The Soviet cosmonaut Yuri Gagarin made the first orbit of the earth on April 12, 1961, in a *Vostok* spacecraft. The trip lasted 108 minutes, and he landed in a field within six miles of the planned descent point. The first orbit by an American was made by John Glenn in a *Mercury* spacecraft on February 20, 1962.

Glenn was not the first American in space, for Alan Shepard had made a "space-hop" on May 5, 1961. He reached an altitude of about 112 miles before returning to earth. Not long after this, on August 6, the Soviet cosmonaut Herman Titov made 17 orbits around the earth.

Both nations spent the next few years practicing linkups in space between independent satellites. This was a difficult task to accomplish, but on March 16, 1966, an American *Gemini* craft linked with an unmanned satellite. The first linkup between two manned satellites took place between the Soviet *Soyuz 4* and *5* spacecraft on January 16, 1969.

▼WHEN DID THE SPACE SHUTTLE MAKE ITS FIRST FLIGHT?

The first space shuttle launch took place on April 12, 1981, using the vehicle *Columbia*. A second shuttle, *Challenger*, made its maiden flight on April 4, 1983. Since their first launchings, both shuttles have been used for further flights. A third craft, *Discovery*, had its maiden voyage on August 30, 1984.

The first launch of *Columbia* was only a test flight. In the hands of commander John Young and pilot Robert Crippen, it made 36 orbits of the earth during its 54-hour stay in space. *Columbia's* launch was scheduled for April 10, but it was delayed for two days. As a result, it took off exactly 20 years after the first orbital flight by Yuri Gagarin.

The main problem encountered during this maiden flight was the loss of some of *Columbia's* 29,000 heat-resistant "tiles." These protect the craft's body from the heat of re-entry into the earth's atmosphere.

On the next flight, on November 12, 1981, instruments were carried in the cargo bay. These were exposed to space when the craft reached its orbit.

ARTS AND SPORT

▼WHEN WERE COLUMNS FIRST USED IN BUILDINGS?

The ancient Egyptians used columns in their temples and tombs as long ago as 2700 B.C. The columns were of several different styles, with a variety of decorations.

The word "column" refers to the whole vertical support, including the base, shaft and the decorated top known as the capital. The simplest form of support used by the Egyptians was a square pillar, often decorated with painting or carving. There was also the Palm column – a smooth cylinder with palm-leaf decorations on the capital.

Bud and Bell columns represented bundles of papyrus reeds tied together. The papyrus was the emblem of Lower Egypt.

▼WHEN WERE THE FIRST THEATERS BUILT?

The first known theaters of a permanent type were built by the ancient Greeks in about the 5th century B.C. We know that the theater of Dionysus in Athens was founded about 500 B.C., although it was rebuilt in 330 B.C. It could hold about 18,000 spectators.

Every important Greek town had its theater, and the early theaters were built in a hollow or bowl shape in a hillside. The spectators sat on stone seats on the hill slope. They looked down on a central, circular area where the performance took place. This area was called an orchestra, and usually had a beaten earth surface.

In time the Greeks added a scene building, closing off the back of the orchestra from the spectators' view. Even later, from 330 B.C. onward, a structure called a proscenium was added in front of the scene building. The proscenium roof was used as a place where the actors could stand to speak. This was the beginning of the use of a stage for performance.

▼WHEN WAS THE ARCH FIRST USED?

The arch was first used by the people of Mesopotamia 5,000 years ago. They built in brick, and invented forms like the true arch, instead of using great stone horizontal roofing slabs, like the Egyptians.

The true arch is a curve of wedge-shaped blocks, known as voussoirs, built over an opening. It is made so that the curve of blocks holds together even when it is only supported at the two sides.

The Egyptians knew of this true arch principle very early on. They did not use it for stone buildings, although they often used it in simple brick buildings.

The arch was introduced into Europe much later by the Etruscans, from about 750 B.C. onward. They developed it in stone, and it was from them that the Romans learned how to build it, and developed it even further. The massive semicircular arches built by the Romans can still be seen in bridges, aqueducts and triumphal arches.

▼WHEN WERE VAULTS FIRST USED IN BUILDINGS?

A vault is an arched covering over a building, made in brick or stone. It developed from the arch, for it is really a continuous series of arches. Like the arch, it was first used in Mesopotamia from 3000 B.C. onward.

The brick barrel-vault was the typical Mesopotamian roof. It was also used in brick buildings by the Egyptians, but not in stonework.

The Romans extended the use of the vault, just as they had made the arch into an important form of building. Their construction of vaults developed particularly after they invented concrete, which they made from volcanic ash, lime, fragments of stone, and water. They were then able to build vaults as much as 80 feet across. This kind of span was not achieved again until steel was used for building in the 19th century. The Romans also began the use of two intersecting barrel-vaults – a groin vault.

▼WHEN DID BUILDINGS FIRST HAVE DOMES?

Domes were first used in the ancient Near East, the Mediterranean area and India. In these very early forms, they were either solid spherical mounds, or used only on small buildings. It was the Romans who developed a way of using them as roofs in large buildings.

Roman methods of making domes developed directly from their construction of the arch and the vault. This is because, in its simplest form, a dome can be built as a series of arches all with the same center. The Romans used concrete and stone to build domes, or "cupolas," as they were also called. One of the earliest examples of a domed building is the Pantheon in Rome. It was built around A.D. 124 by Emperor Hadrian.

The Romans built domes over circular buildings. Byzantine architects, from about the 5th century onward, improved on Roman techniques. They worked out how to erect domes over square buildings.

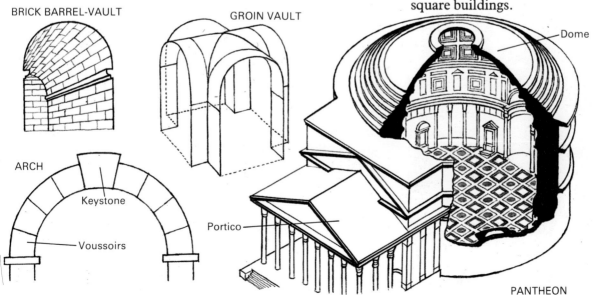

BRICK BARREL-VAULT

GROIN VAULT

ARCH

Keystone

Voussoirs

Portico

Dome

PANTHEON

►WHEN WERE MUSICAL INSTRUMENTS FIRST PLAYED?

Musical instruments have been played since prehistoric times. The earliest instruments were objects such as conches (seashells) and bone pipes, which people could use just as they found them.

Later, instruments were made from materials such as wood and pottery. People found that string can make a musical note when stretched tight, so they made the first musical bow.

In early times, music accompanied dancing and religious ceremonies. People of the ancient civilizations of Mesopotamia, Egypt, India, China and Greece then started to listen to music purely as a way of enjoying themselves.

The picture shows musicians of ancient Egypt. The woman on the left is playing a harp. Next to her is a girl playing a lute. The women on the right are playing a double pipe and a lyre.

▲WHEN DID THE FIRST ORCHESTRAS APPEAR?

An orchestra is a large group of musicians. The first orchestras appeared at the beginning of the 17th century, as part of Italian opera.

Early orchestras varied in the instruments they included. Which ones were used seems to have been determined simply by which musicians were available. The orchestra for Monteverdi's opera *Orfeo*, of 1607, included nearly all the instruments known at that time, except drums.

In 18th-century Germany, composers began to write music for four basic groups of instruments in the orchestra. These were the *woodwinds* (such as flutes, oboes and bassoons), *brass* (horns and trumpets), *percussion* (kettledrums) and *strings* (violins, violas, cellos and double bass). These groups of instruments are still the basis of the modern 20th-century symphony orchestra.

◄WHEN WAS MUSIC FIRST WRITTEN DOWN?

Forms of written music existed in the ancient civilizations of Egypt, Mesopotamia and Greece. Exactly when music was first written down is difficult to say. Our knowlege depends on whether copies of the music survive, or whether there are surviving references to it in pictures and literature.

We know that the Greek philosopher Pythagoras (6th century B.C.) brought a knowledge of musical theory back to Greece after studying in Egypt and Mesopotamia. There is also an example of what experts believe is the musical notation (written music) of a Sumerian hymn dating from between 5,000 and 3,000 years ago. No one has yet deciphered it.

The first written music which survives in a complete form dates from the 9th century. The sheet of music shown here dates from the Middle Ages.

▲WHEN WAS OPERA FIRST PERFORMED?

The beginning of opera is usually dated around 1600 in Italy, when stage plays set to music were first performed.

Works of drama performed to music existed long ago, for example in the Mystery, Miracle and Morality plays of the Middle Ages. These were forms of sacred drama. They arose from traditions begun in the Christian Church as early as the 4th century. There were also types of entertainment for the aristocracy which combined simple plots, poetry and music.

The first full stage play set to music, in which the characters sing, was produced in 1597. Its music has not survived. The first two surviving operas were performed in 1600 in Italy. Both had specially designed costumes, scenery, lighting and stage machinery. Monteverdi was the first great opera composer. His opera *Orfeo* was first performed in 1607.

▲WHEN DID MODERN DANCE APPEAR?

Modern dance developed at the beginning of the 20th century. There were two styles – one in Europe, and one in the United States.

The pioneers of modern dance were dissatisfied with classical ballet. They criticized its themes of romantic fairytales and legend, and thought that it did not explore new ideas.

European modern dance explored ideas about the body in relation to space. American modern dance drew inspiration from other cultures.

Choreographers invented new ballets. Their themes were based on ancient ritual and myth, as well as modern subjects. The themes were the heart of their dances, instead of being just an aid to the techniques of movement.

One of the early American leaders was Isadora Duncan, shown here. She began to experiment at the beginning of this century. She took her ideas, costume and style of dance from the ancient Greeks.

▼WHEN WAS JAZZ FIRST PLAYED?

The style of music known as jazz emerged at the start of the 20th century. It began in the southern states of the U.S., but no one knows exactly when or how it started.

In the southern states, Black slaves had kept the musical traditions of their West African ancestors. They also had their own style of religious songs and music, known as spirituals. Jazz was influenced by both these styles of music.

By the start of the 1900s a distinct type of music had developed in New Orleans, in Louisiana. It was played by Black musicians. The early leaders of this "jazz" music were all trumpeters. They included Joe "King" Oliver and Louis Armstrong.

In 1917 musicians from New Orleans moved north. Some settled in Chicago. By the early 1920s Chicago was the new center of jazz. From there it developed into an international style of music.

◄WHEN WERE THE FIRST SCULPTURES MADE?

The earliest sculptures that have been found are as much as 30,000 years old, dating from the Stone Age. They are tiny figures representing women, which have come to be known as the "Venuses."

Stone Age Venuses have been found all over Europe and western Asia, from the Pyrenees to Lake Baikal in the U.S.S.R. Stone Age sculptors also made figures of animals. These included mammoths, rhinoceroses, horses, cave bears and various kinds of cat.

Stone Age sculptors worked in a variety of materials. They used ivory from mammoth tusks, as well as bone and stone such as limestone and sandstone. They also made terracotta figures from a mixture of clay, powdered bone and some kind of fat, possibly animal fat.

The stone sculpture in the picture shows two people embracing. It was made in Jordan 12,000 years ago.

►WHEN WERE THE FIRST WATERCOLORS PAINTED?

The use of watercolor in painting has a long history. We know that watercolor paint was used on papyrus rolls in ancient Egypt, and in the earliest paintings of China.

Watercolor is a paint ground in gum (usually gum arabic), which can be dissolved in water. It is usually applied with a brush.

Drawings in watercolor and ink have been the basis of Chinese art since the beginning of the T'ang Dynasty in A.D. 618. During this period the traditions and techniques of Chinese landscape painting were developing.

Chinese pictures were usually painted on silk, or sometimes paper, mainly in the form of scrolls. These could be hung on a wall or rolled up for storing away. Some paintings were also made on walls or folding screens and panels. The figure shown here was painted by Hsiang Kun in the 2nd century A.D.

◄WHEN WAS PERSPECTIVE FIRST USED IN EUROPEAN PAINTING?

Perspective is a method of drawing a picture so as to give an impression of realistic depth and distance. The laws of perspective were worked out and first used in the 15th century in Italy.

The Italian architect Brunelleschi worked out the principles of perspective. These are based on the fact that objects seem smaller the closer they are to the horizon. Brunelleschi's friend Masaccio first applied these ideas to painting in a fresco (wall painting) finished in 1427. The use of perspective gave a totally new approach to painting. It was followed by European artists for 500 years.

The picture shows the dramatic use of perspective. It is a detail from *The Flagellation*, a painting made by Piero della Francesca in about 1460. Piero carefully worked out the perspective of the building and figures.

▶WHEN DID JAPANESE PRINTS BECOME WORLD-FAMOUS?

Japanese color prints in the style known as *ukiyo-e* were first seen in Europe in the second half of the 19th century. They have influenced many European artists since then.

Ukiyo-e is a style of art which arose in the 16th and 17th centuries to appeal to popular tastes. It continued until the mid-19th century. Some of the works best known in Europe are the landscape prints of Hokusai.

Early *ukiyo-e* prints showed city life and theater scenes. Later, illustrations of warrior

legends became very popular. From 1765 onwards, prints of birds, animals, flowers and landscapes were produced.

The print shown here is by Kunisada. It shows Japanese gods dancing in front of Amaterasu, the sun goddess.

▼WHEN DID AFRICAN ART INFLUENCE EUROPEAN PAINTING?

The painter Picasso came into contact with African art in 1906-07. It totally altered his ideas of how to paint solid objects on a flat surface. In 1907 he started to paint *Les

***Demoiselles d'Avignon* ("The Young Ladies of Avignon"), shown here. From this developed the style known as Cubism, which completely changed the course of 20th-century art.**

For 500 years artists had shown their subjects realistically, from a single viewpoint, using the laws of perspective. Picasso saw that African sculpture had the key to how artists could escape from this rigid approach.

African sculptors express ideas about their subjects instead of showing them in a realistic way. The human head and body are often broken down and shown in an abstract, symbolic way.

Picasso and other Cubist painters abandoned the use of traditional perspective. They began to paint works in which an object is seen from several viewpoints as a fragmented single image.

▲WHEN WAS POLO FIRST PLAYED?

▲WHEN WERE BALL GAMES FIRST PLAYED?

▲WHEN WAS BASKETBALL FIRST PLAYED?

Polo is a game played on horseback with a mallet and ball. It is the oldest of all the sports which use horses. We know that people played polo in Persia (Iran) in the 1st century A.D., and it is believed that the Persians invented it.

Polo started as a game used in training cavalry units of the king's guard and other mounted troops. It then became a national sport known as *chaugan*, meaning "mallet," or "stick." *Chaugan* was played a great deal by the men and women of Persian noble families.

The game spread to Arabia, Tibet, China and Japan. Muslims took it to India in the 13th century A.D. It was in India that polo was first played by Europeans – by some British tea planters who formed the first European polo club in 1859. The game quickly became very popular among the British in India. It was first played in England in 1870, and in the U.S. in 1876.

Ball games are one of the oldest games played by people. There is evidence in early art that they have been played since prehistoric times.

The ancient Egyptians, the Greeks and the Romans are all known to have enjoyed ball games. They are mentioned in early writings and shown in art, for example on Egyptian monuments.

The Greeks believed that ball play was particularly useful for developing grace and suppleness in the body. The Romans had an area for ball games in Roman baths, and wealthy Romans even had private ball courts in their villas. They used balls made of leather.

Many of the earliest games we know about consisted of no more than throwing the ball from player to player. There were few rules. But we know that team games and competitions of various kinds were also played by the ancient Greeks, particularly the Spartans.

Basketball was played for the first time in December 1891, in the U.S. It was invented by James Naismith at an International Young Men's Christian Association training school.

Naismith was asked to devise a new game to inspire the students. They were bored with their daily physical education class. He used ideas from games such as hockey, football and soccer, blended them with his own ideas, and invented basketball.

The bored students at the YMCA quickly became interested. News of the game spread rapidly to other parts of the U.S. During the next ten years it was introduced into Canada, France, Britain, China, India and Japan.

The first goals were two peach baskets. The iron hoop and net was introduced two years later. People had to climb a ladder to get the ball from the net. Cutting a hole in the net so that the ball could drop through came later.

Kendo

Judo

Karate

kicking, throwing, choking and holding an opponent.

Typical martial arts are judo, karate, aikido, sumo and kendo. Judo is a form of jacket wrestling based on *jiujitsu* methods. It was started in 1882 by Jigoro Kano, who founded the first school of judo. Sumo (belt wrestling) also began with the *samurai*.

Karate is a way of fighting without weapons. It was developed over several centuries, probably by people who were forbidden to carry weapons. It became a sport in the 1920s.

Aikido is a system of self-defense designed to subdue the opponent. Kendo, a form of fencing, began in the 18th century as sword-fighting practice. Light bamboo swords were used so that the *samurai* could fence without injuring each other.

▲WHEN DID THE MARTIAL ARTS FIRST DEVELOP?

The martial arts are methods of self-defense and combat. They began in Japan and evolved into sports at the end of the 19th century and beginning of the 20th century. They are based on techniques which are centuries old, such as those of *jiujitsu*.

Jiujitsu is a way of fighting hand to hand, using as few weapons as possible. It was developed by the warrior class, or *samurai*, in Japan from the 17th century onward. *Jiujitsu* involves methods of hitting,

▼WHEN DID THE FIRST AUTOMOBILE RACES TAKE PLACE?

The first automobile race was in 1895 in France. The winner was Emile Levassor, who **drove a French Panhard. He did more than 48 hours driving at an average speed of 15 miles an hour.**

There had been informal contests between "horseless carriages" from the 1880s onward, as this was a way of proving how safe and fast the automobiles were. The first formal race took place in France in June 1895, run from Paris to Bordeaux and back. Soon after, there were races from Paris to Vienna, and from Paris to Berlin.

These races were dangerous events. Dogs and farm carts had to be avoided on bad roads. The driver's vision was sometimes totally obscured by clouds of dust. But these harsh tests of the cars also led to better cars being made.

An international series of races began in 1900, arranged by an American called James Gordon Bennett. They were followed by the Grand Prix series, begun in 1906 by French car makers. These still take place every year.

INDEX

Page numbers in *italics* refer to pictures

PHOTOGRAPHIC ACKNOWLEDGEMENTS

Pages: 29 Louvre, 31 Michael Holford, 32 Sonia Halliday Photos/
F.H.C.Birch, 38 Zefa, 40 Sonia Halliday, 44 Burger Bibliothek,
Bern, 45 Scala, 48 Mansell, 49 Michael Holford, 57 Mansell,
61 Kyoto Costume Institute, 62 Scala, 63 Popperfoto, 65 top
Novosti Press Agency, bottom BBC Hulton Picture Library, 66
Keystone, 67 Mansell, 68 Zefa, 69 Popperfoto, 70 & 71 Michael
Holford, 72 Zefa, 73 & 79 top BBC Hulton Picture Library, 79
bottom Bettmann Archive/Hulton, 80 Kodak Museum, 82 top BBC
Hulton Picture Library, 82 middle Design Council, 82 bottom &
83 Mansell, 84 left Bettmann Archive/ Hulton, 84 right Marconi
Radar, 85 top Public Record Office, 85 bottom Hughes Aircraft Co,
87 Sonia Halliday, 89 & 92 BBC Hulton Picture Library, 93 top
National Motor Museum, 93 middle Mansell, 95 Union Pacific Rail-
road Museum, 104 top Scala, 104 bottom & 105 National Maritime
Museum, 107 Zefa, 108 left Robert Harding, 108 right U.S. Naval
Observatory, 110 Mansell, 111 Nasa, 114 Fotomas Indes, 116 top
The British Museum, 116 middle Michael Holford, 116 bottom Scala,
117 top Michael Holford, 117 bottom Museum of Modern Art, New
York.

Picture Research: Penny J. Warn.